PHX 11/21

THE ULTIMATE BOOK OF
SPACE

Claudia Martin

Consultant: Martin Redfern

ARCTURUS

Picture Credits:
Every attempt has been made to clear copyright. Should there be any inadvertent omission, please apply to the publisher for rectification.
Key: b–bottom, t–top, c–center, l–left, r–right

ARCTURUS

This edition published in 2021 by Arcturus Publishing Limited
26/27 Bickels Yard, 151–153 Bermondsey Street,
London SE1 3HA

Copyright © Arcturus Holdings Limited

ISBN: 978-1-83940-597-6
CH007795US
Supplier 29, Date 0421, Print run 10826

Printed in China

Author: Claudia Martin
Designer: Lorraine Inglis
Picture research: Paul Futcher
Consultant: Martin Redfern

A note on numbers:
1 million = 1,000,000
1 billion = 1,000,000,000
1 trillion = 1 followed by 12 zeros
1 quadrillion = 1 followed by 15 zeros
1 quintillion = 1 followed by 18 zeros
1 sextillion = 1 followed by 21 zeros
1 septillion = 1 followed by 24 zeros
1 octillion = 1 followed by 27 zeros
1 nonillion = 1 followed by 30 zeros

THE ULTIMATE BOOK OF
SPACE
CONTENTS

Understanding the Universe

Earth is one of eight planets that move in a roughly circular path around a medium-sized star, known as the Sun. The Sun is one of up to 400 billion stars in our spiral-shaped galaxy, the Milky Way. This galaxy is one of perhaps 2 trillion galaxies in the Universe, which—as far as we can know—contains everything that exists.

When ancient peoples looked at the night sky, they could tell apart the shining, slowly moving stars from the five closest planets, which they watched moving in unexplained patterns. Until the 16th century, most people—if they considered their place in the Universe at all—believed the Earth was at the heart of the Universe, with the Sun, stars, and planets moving round us. Most people had no idea that the Sun itself was a star, just like many of the bright lights in the night sky.

Discovery by discovery, our understanding of the Universe grew. Mathematicians made the first leaps, when they calculated distances to the Moon and Sun. From 1608, the invention of the telescope enabled us to see the moons of other planets and, eventually, to focus on distant clouds of gas where new stars were forming or dying. During the 19th century, we learned how to measure the energy released by stars and galaxies, enabling us to piece together what they are made of. After 1957, we were able to launch spacecraft to study the farthest reaches of the Solar System and even beyond.

Having noticed in 1929 that distant galaxies are moving away from us, we realized that the Universe is growing. Calculating backward, we came to the understanding that the Universe started to grow from a tiny point 13.8 billion years ago—but we may never understand why.

Saturn is the most distant planet that can be seen from Earth without a telescope. Through a small telescope, rings made of icy and rocky chunks can be seen around its equator.

The Butterfly Nebula is a cloud of glowing gas thrown out by a dying star. The nebula is so far away that its light has taken 3,400 years to reach us.

INNER SOLAR SYSTEM

The Solar System is all the objects that orbit (or travel around) the star we call the Sun. The region nearest the Sun, within about 500 million km (310 million miles), is the Inner Solar System. Here are the planets Mercury, Venus, Earth, and Mars, surrounded by a ring of rocky objects called the Asteroid Belt.

The Solar System includes eight planets, at least five dwarf planets, and other objects including moons, comets, and asteroids. A planet is an object that is in orbit around a star, is nearly round, and is large enough to push or pull other objects out of its path. The only large objects orbiting close to a planet are its own moons. Moons are objects that orbit a planet rather than directly around a star. Dwarf planets, such as the Inner Solar System's Ceres, are too small to clear their orbit, so other large objects can be found nearby.

When the Solar System was forming, lighter materials and gases were blown away from the Sun into the Outer Solar System. While the outer planets are large and gassy, the inner planets are smaller and made of heavier materials: metals and rock. The inner planets are known as terrestrial (or "Earth-like") planets because they all contain similar materials to Earth. Unlike the outer planets, the inner planets have few or no moons and no ring systems.

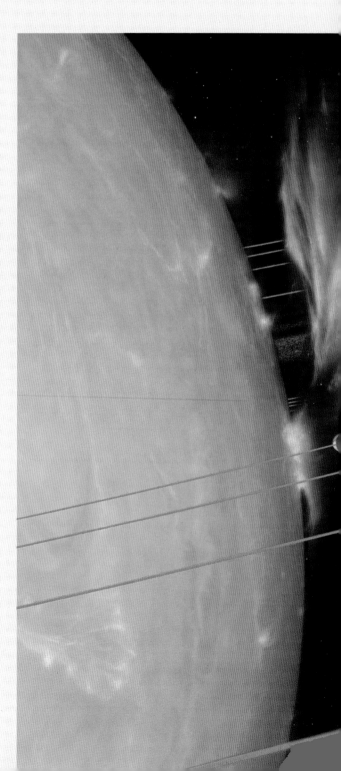

The smallest planet in the Solar System, just 4,880 km (3,032 miles) across, is also the closest to the Sun: Mercury.

Sun　Mercury　Earth　Mars
Venus

Gravity

All the objects in the Solar System are held in orbit around the Sun by gravity. Gravity is a force that pulls all objects toward each other. The greater an object's mass (or weight), the greater the pull of its gravity. Since the Sun is the heaviest object in the Solar System, all the other objects are in motion around it. All the larger objects are moving in roughly circular, counterclockwise paths around the Sun, as if moving across a nearly flat plate.

The English scientist Sir Isaac Newton (1642–1727) worked out mathematical rules that explained how every particle in the Universe attracts every other particle with its gravity.

From closest to the Sun to most distant, the planets of the Solar System are: Mercury, Venus, Earth, Mars, Jupiter, Saturn, Uranus, and Neptune. Earth has one moon, while Mars has two.

The planets of the Inner Solar System form in a disk of gas and dust that is spinning around the young Sun.

THE SOLAR SYSTEM

Our Solar System was born around 4.57 billion years ago. First, a clump formed in a vast cloud of dust and gas. The clump grew bigger, its gravity pulling more material toward it. Most of the material formed the Sun, while the rest flattened into a spinning plate of gas and dust called a protoplanetary disk. All the planets and moons formed from the disk.

As more and more material was pulled into the forming Sun, the pressure at its heart became so great that hydrogen atoms began to join together, forming a new type of atom: helium. Atoms, a million times thinner than a human hair, are the building blocks for every material in the Universe. As hydrogen atoms smash together, they release huge amounts of energy. This made the Sun start to glow with heat and light—just as our star still does today.

In the protoplanetary disk, more clumps started to form. These bumped into each other, forming bigger clumps. Some grew large enough for their own gravity to pull them into ball shapes, called spheres. Other small pieces of material were not able to join together, instead forming the rocky objects of the Asteroid Belt or comets.

As material was pulled into the planets of the Inner Solar System, the new planets were squeezed so tightly they became very hot. Heavy materials, such as the metals iron and nickel, melted and sank to the planets' cores. Lighter materials rose to the surface and made oceans of liquid rock. It was millions of years before the planets' surfaces cooled into solid rock.

Earth formed around 4.54 billion years ago. For as long as the first 500 million years, Earth was too hot for any form of life.

Early in their lives, all the inner planets were battered by space rocks, called asteroids.

The Solar System

Type: Planetary system

Size: 27 billion km (16.8 billion miles) across

Mass: 1.0014 Suns (the Sun weighs 2 nonillion kg, or 2 followed by 30 zeros)

Known planets: 8

Age: 4.57 million years

Distance from Middle of Milky Way Galaxy: 27,000 light years (for light years, see page 127)

EARTH

Earth is the largest of the inner planets. The third planet from the Sun, it receives enough warmth from the star for water to flow on its surface. If Earth were hotter, water would boil. If it were colder, all water would freeze. Without water, there would be no life. As far as we currently know, Earth is the only planet in the Universe that is home to life.

As Earth orbits the Sun, it also rotates round its own axis, an invisible line through the planet's core from the North Pole to the South Pole. Earth rotates eastward, with each rotation taking 24 hours. When one side of Earth is facing the Sun, it experiences day, while the other experiences night. Earth's axis is tilted slightly in relation to its orbit around the Sun. This means that—apart from on the equator—nowhere experiences exactly 12 hours of day and 12 hours of night all the time.

It takes 365.25 days for Earth to orbit the Sun. Since this is longer than the 365-day year we use in our calendars, we have a leap year with 366 days every four years, to keep pace. The tilt of Earth's axis creates seasons. When the North Pole is tilted toward the Sun, the planet's northern regions experience summer while the southern regions have winter.

Earth's crust of solid rock is broken into giant plates, called tectonic plates. These move very slowly on the partly melted rock below. As the plates move against each other, they can slowly push up rock, forming mountains. Melted rock can surge up at the edges of plates, forming volcanoes.

Solid metal inner core

Rocky mantle

Solid rock crust

Liquid metal outer core

Earth's inner core of iron and nickel reaches 5,200°C (9,400°F), but is squeezed so tightly that it is solid. The outer core is liquid metal. The mantle is a layer of hot, partly melted rock, while the crust is cool, solid rock.

Earth

Type: Terrestrial planet

Size: 12,742 km (7,918 miles) across

Mass: 0.000003 Suns

Moons: 1

Year: 365.25 days

Day: 24 hours

Surface Temperature: -89.2–56.7°C (-128.6–134°F)

Average Distance from the Sun: 149.6 million km (93 million miles)

Electric currents in the flowing iron and nickel of Earth's outer core create magnetism, a force that attracts and repels similar metals. This makes Earth a giant magnet, which is why a magnetic compass needle always points northward.

This photograph of Earth was taken by the *Lunar Reconnaissance Orbiter* robotic spacecraft when it was 134 km (83 miles) above the Moon's Compton Crater, which lies just on the far side of the Moon.

EARTH'S ATMOSPHERE

Earth's atmosphere is a mixture of gases, often called air, which is held around the planet by its gravity. Without the atmosphere, there would be no life on Earth. It gives us oxygen, which all animals need to survive, as well as rain to drink and to water plants. The atmosphere acts like a blanket, trapping just enough heat from the Sun to keep us warm.

The atmosphere contains around 78 percent nitrogen, 21 percent oxygen, and small amounts of argon, carbon dioxide, and other gases. Moving up through the atmosphere, the air becomes thinner. Scientists divide the atmosphere into layers, depending on their temperature. Although the air largely gets colder farther from Earth, both the thermosphere and stratosphere layers are warmed by energy they absorb from the Sun.

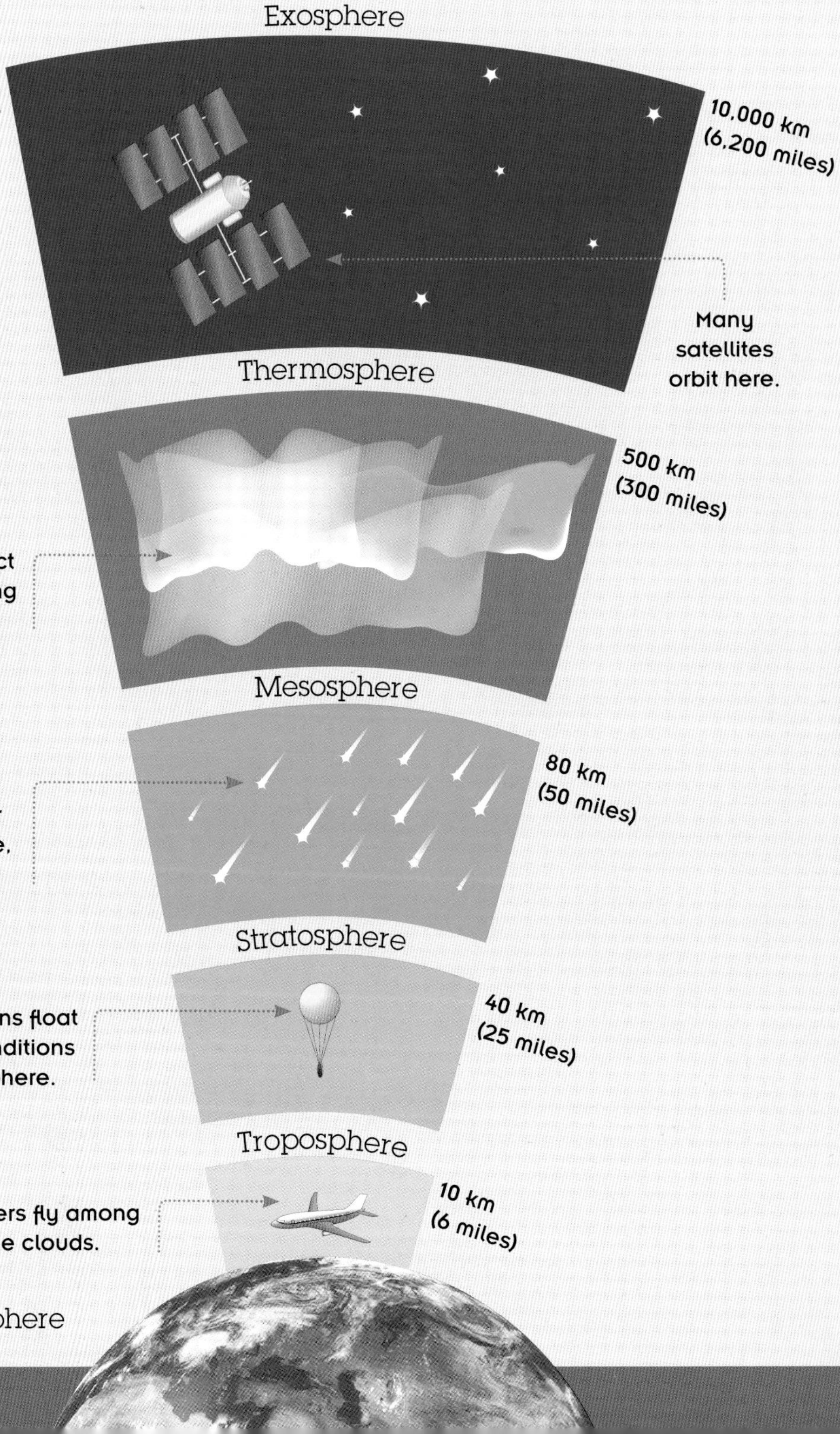

Energy-carrying particles from the Sun interact with the Earth's magnetic field, creating glowing lights called aurorae around the poles.

Meteoroids, which are small rocky or metal bodies that enter Earth's atmosphere, burn up here, creating "shooting stars."

Weather balloons float to measure conditions in the atmosphere.

Airliners fly among the clouds.

Exosphere

10,000 km (6,200 miles)

Many satellites orbit here.

Thermosphere

500 km (300 miles)

Mesosphere

80 km (50 miles)

Stratosphere

40 km (25 miles)

Troposphere

10 km (6 miles)

Layers of the atmosphere

When the Sun heats lakes and oceans, some water evaporates. It becomes an invisible gas, which rises in the warm air. As the air rises, it cools. Cold air cannot hold as much evaporated water as warm air, so some of it condenses back into water drops, which we see as a cloud. When the water drops get too heavy to float, they fall as rain. This process is called the water cycle.

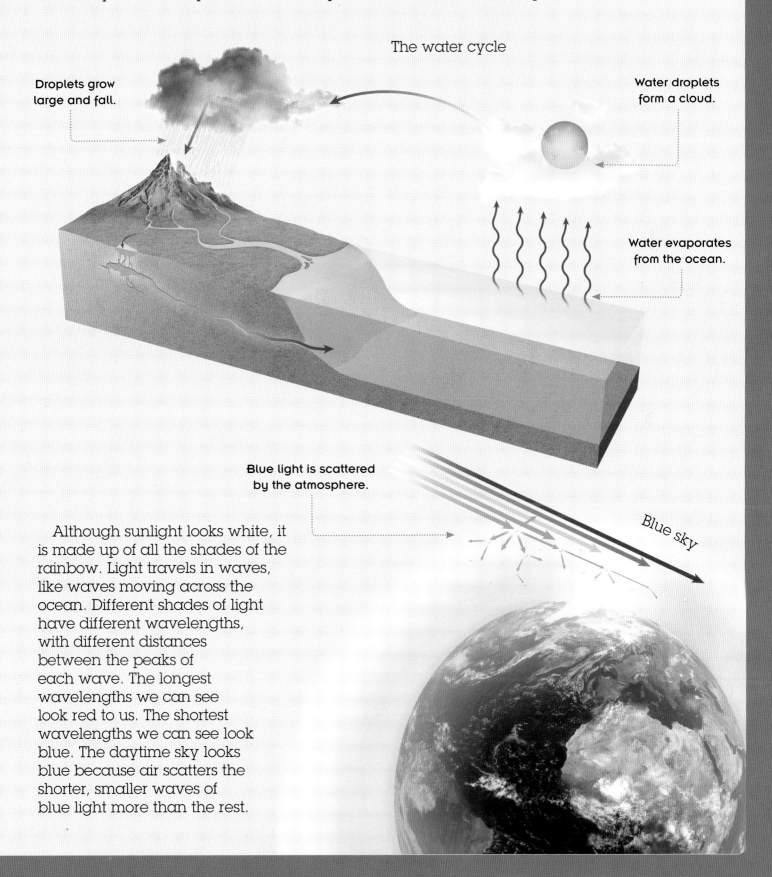

The water cycle

Droplets grow large and fall.

Water droplets form a cloud.

Water evaporates from the ocean.

Blue light is scattered by the atmosphere.

Blue sky

Although sunlight looks white, it is made up of all the shades of the rainbow. Light travels in waves, like waves moving across the ocean. Different shades of light have different wavelengths, with different distances between the peaks of each wave. The longest wavelengths we can see look red to us. The shortest wavelengths we can see look blue. The daytime sky looks blue because air scatters the shorter, smaller waves of blue light more than the rest.

The bright impact crater to the left of the middle of the Moon's near side is called Copernicus. Above the crater is the vast Mare Imbrium ("Sea of Rains").

THE MOON

Earth has one moon, the fifth largest in the Solar System after moons belonging to Jupiter and Saturn. The Moon has orbited our planet for around 4.51 billion years, since about 30 million years after Earth formed. The Moon's orbit is elliptical (or oval), so its distance from Earth ranges from 356,400 km (221,500 miles) to 406,700 km (252,700 miles).

Astronomers believe the Moon formed after a Mars-sized planet crashed into the young Earth, sending material shooting into Earth's orbit. This material pulled together into the Moon. The Moon has a partly melted core of iron, a mantle of hot rock, and a crust of cool rock. It has almost no atmosphere.

As the Moon orbits Earth, it also rotates on its axis. Since the Moon takes the same time—27.3 days—to rotate on its axis as it does to travel round Earth, it always shows the same side, known as the near side, to Earth. A day on the Moon lasts 29.5 Earth days, because if an astronaut were standing on the Moon it would take 29.5 days for them to see the Sun appear to move across the sky and back to its original position. This is longer than the time taken for the Moon to rotate, because the Earth is moving around the Sun at the same time.

From Earth, we can see dark areas on the Moon's surface. These formed billions of years ago when volcanoes released floods of melted rock, called magma, which cooled and hardened. These areas are called maria (from the Latin for "seas") because people once thought they were filled with water. We can also see bright impact craters where asteroids or comets have broken the Moon's surface.

The Moon probably formed when a planet, which astronomers call Theia, careered into Earth.

The Moon

Type: Moon

Size: 3,476 km (2,160 miles) across

Mass: 0.012 Earths

Year: 365.25 Earth days

Day: 29.5 Earth days

Surface Temperature: -272–127°C (-458–260°F)

Average Distance from Earth: 384,402 km (238,856 miles)

Pull of the Moon's gravity

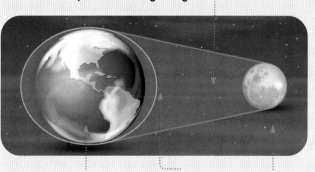

Earth   High tide   Moon

The Moon's gravity pulls Earth's oceans, creating tides when the water rises up and draws back on the shore as the Moon moves around Earth.

PHASES OF THE MOON

The Moon is the second brightest object in our sky, after the Sun, because its surface reflects the Sun's light. The Sun lights up the side of the Moon that faces it. Yet as the Moon orbits Earth and Earth orbits the Sun, we see different amounts of the Moon's bright side. These changes are known as the Moon's phases.

When the Moon is between the Sun and Earth, the Sun's light shines on its far side, which we cannot see. From Earth, the Moon appears invisible or as a very thin crescent. This is called a new moon. When the Moon is on the opposite side of Earth from the Sun, sunlight shines on the whole of the near side. This is called a full moon. The rest of the time, we see parts of the Moon's sunlit face. The cycle repeats every 29.5 days, when the Moon returns to its original position in relation to the Sun, as seen by someone on Earth.

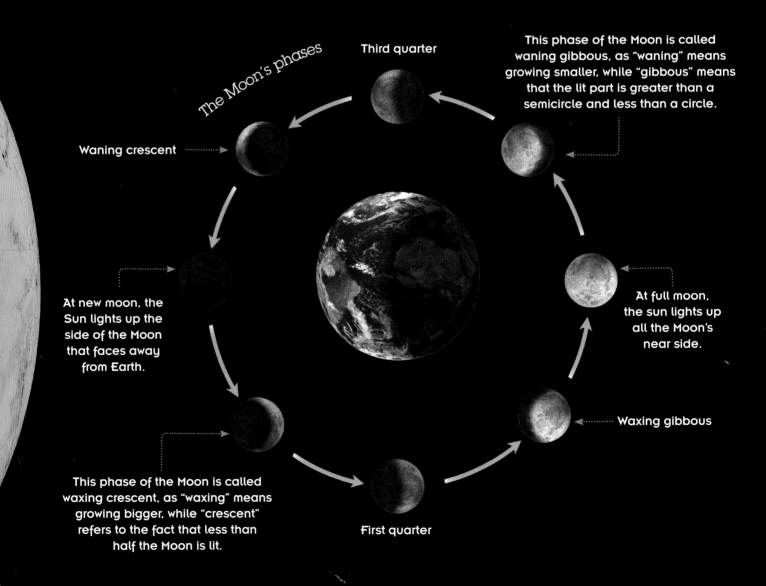

The Moon's phases

Third quarter

This phase of the Moon is called waning gibbous, as "waning" means growing smaller, while "gibbous" means that the lit part is greater than a semicircle and less than a circle.

Waning crescent

At new moon, the Sun lights up the side of the Moon that faces away from Earth.

At full moon, the sun lights up all the Moon's near side.

Waxing gibbous

This phase of the Moon is called waxing crescent, as "waxing" means growing bigger, while "crescent" refers to the fact that less than half the Moon is lit.

First quarter

A lunar eclipse is when the Moon is in the Earth's shadow. This happens when the Sun, Earth, and Moon are in a straight line, with the Moon on the opposite side of Earth from the Sun. The Moon does not completely darken even during a total eclipse, as it receives some sunlight that has been refracted (or bent) by Earth's atmosphere. A total lunar eclipse happens about twice every 3 years.

Total lunar eclipse

The Moon's face appears reddish because, after the Sun's light has been bent and scattered, the wavelengths that we see as red remain.

Total solar eclipse

Total solar eclipses are rare because the Moon is often too far from Earth to block the Sun entirely.

A solar eclipse is when the Moon blocks the face of the Sun, when the Sun, Moon, and Earth are exactly lined up. Total solar eclipses last for a few minutes and can be seen from somewhere on Earth around once every 18 months. Since looking at the Sun can cause blindness, a solar eclipse should never be watched directly or through a camera.

MERCURY

The closest planet to the Sun, Mercury has the quickest orbit: 87.97 Earth days. When viewed from Earth, Mercury is so close to the Sun that it is lost in its glare most of the time. Mercury can only be seen—as a star-like light—just after sunset or before sunrise. Along with Venus, Mars, Jupiter, and Saturn, Mercury was recognized as a planet in ancient times.

Mercury has almost no atmosphere to keep it warm, so it has a greater difference between its daytime and night-time temperatures than any other planet in the Solar System. It ranges from 427°C (800°F) during the day, when it is baked by the Sun, to -173°C (-280°F) at night.

Low-lying areas of the planet are filled by cooled magma that leaked from the mantle in the distant past. Later in the planet's life, as it cooled, its surface cracked and formed ridges, a little like the skin on cooling milk. Mercury's surface is also marked by many impact craters.

Never less than 77 million km (48 million miles) from Earth, Mercury has been visited by only two robotic spacecraft: *Mariner 10*, which flew past in 1974–5, and *MESSENGER*, which orbited in 2011–15. It is difficult for a spacecraft to orbit Mercury, because, as the craft nears the Sun, it is sped up by the pull of the Sun's gravity. To be captured instead by Mercury's gravity, it must slow down dramatically.

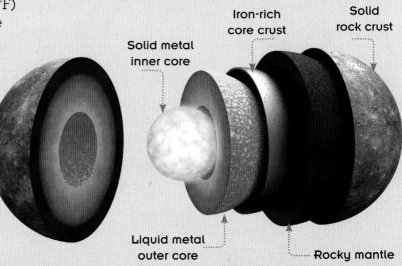

Solid metal inner core

Iron-rich core crust

Solid rock crust

Liquid metal outer core

Rocky mantle

Like Earth, Mercury has a rocky crust and mantle, with a core of metal. However, Mercury's core takes up much more of its interior than Earth's, occupying more than half its volume.

Mercury

Type: Terrestrial planet

Size: 4,880 km (3,032 miles) across

Mass: 0.055 Earths

Moons: 0

Year: 87.97 Earth days

Day: 176 Earth days

Surface Temperature: -173–427°C (-280–800°F)

Average Distance from the Sun: 57.9 million km (36 million miles)

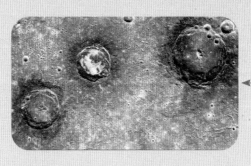

MESSENGER captured this image of three of Mercury's impact craters, named Munch, Sander, and Poe after an artist, photographer, and author.

This image, based on maps made by *MESSENGER*, uses blues and creams to show the different rocks on Mercury's surface. In reality, Mercury is brownish.

The space probe *Magellan* mapped Venus in 1990–94 using radar, a system that bounced radio waves off the planet's surface and measured how long they took to return.

VENUS

Venus has a similar size, mass (or weight), and structure to Earth. However, its atmosphere is very different from Earth's, since it contains 96 percent carbon dioxide. This gas traps the Sun's heat, making Venus the hottest planet in the Solar System. The temperature on the planet's surface is hot enough to melt metals such as lead and tin.

Venus's atmosphere is much denser (or tightly packed) than Earth's. If it were possible to stand on Venus's baking surface, the atmosphere would press down 92 times more heavily than Earth's atmosphere. It would feel like being 1 km (0.6 miles) beneath the ocean surface. Rather than having clouds of water drops, Venus has a thick layer of clouds of sulfuric acid drops. The planet may once have had an atmosphere more like Earth's, along with oceans of water. As the atmosphere gained more carbon dioxide and heated up, the oceans would have boiled and evaporated.

Venus turns on its axis once every 243 Earth days, giving it a slower rotation than any other Solar System planet. It also rotates in the opposite direction from every planet apart from Uranus. This means that, on Venus, the Sun rises in the west and sets in the east. It is possible that Venus was either flipped over at some point, or its rotation slowed to a standstill before starting to turn the opposite way.

Solid rock crust

Rocky mantle

Metal core

Venus's core is probably partly melted iron and nickel.

Venus

Type: Terrestrial planet

Size: 12,104 km (7,521 miles) across

Mass: 0.815 Earths

Moons: 0

Year: 224.7 Earth days

Day: 117 Earth days

Surface Temperature: 460°C (860°F)

Average Distance from the Sun: 108.2 million km (67.2 million miles)

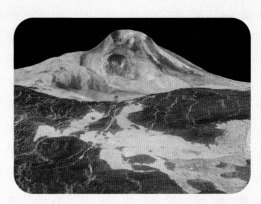

Magellan created this image of Maat Mons, an 8-km (5-mile) high volcano. Venus has 1,600 major volcanoes, more than any other planet in the Solar System.

MARS

Mars was named after the Roman god of war. All the Solar System planets, apart from Earth, were named after a Roman or Greek god. Mars is also known as the "Red Planet" because of the rusty dust in its atmosphere, making it look red from Earth. The rocks of the planet's crust contain lots of iron oxide, which on Earth forms rust on the surface of iron.

Mars is smaller and less dense than Earth. This makes its mass smaller—and its gravity less strong—than Earth's. If an astronaut were to stand on Mars's surface (which has not yet happened), they would be able to jump three times higher than on Earth.

Mars has been visited by dozens of uncrewed spacecraft, starting with the flyby of the USA's *Mariner 4* in 1965. In 1971, the Soviet Union's *Mars 2* became the first lander to reach the planet's surface. The first robotic rover to roll across the surface was the USA's *Sojourner*, in 1997.

Scientists study whether there may once have been life on Mars. Mars's atmosphere is very thin, so it barely presses down on the planet's surface and any liquid water would drift away. However, scientists believe that, more than 3.8 billion years ago, the atmosphere was much thicker. Water may have flowed across the planet's surface, perhaps filling an ocean where life could have developed, as it did on Earth. Today, there is still some water on Mars, but it is frozen at the planet's poles.

Metal core

Solid rock crust

Rocky mantle

Mars has a core of iron and nickel, around 3,588 km (2,230 miles) wide, surrounded by a rock mantle and crust.

Mars

Type: Terrestrial planet

Size: 6,779 km (4,212 miles) across

Mass: 0.107 Earths

Moons: 2

Year: 687 Earth days

Day: 24.65 Earth hours

Surface Temperature: -153–20°C (-243–68°F)

Average Distance from the Sun: 227.9 million km (141.6 million miles)

This illustration shows Mars's two small moons, Phobos and Deimos, which may be asteroids that were captured by the planet's gravity.

The ice of Mars's North Pole shines white, while volcanoes, canyons, and impact craters dot the planet's surface.

THE ASTEROID BELT

The Asteroid Belt is a ring-shaped region between the orbits of Mars and Jupiter where millions of rocky and metal objects, called asteroids, are orbiting the Sun. Most of the asteroids are tiny, but at least 1 million are over 1 km (0.6 miles) wide. The four largest asteroids—Ceres, Vesta, Pallas, and Hygiea—make up about half the weight of the whole belt.

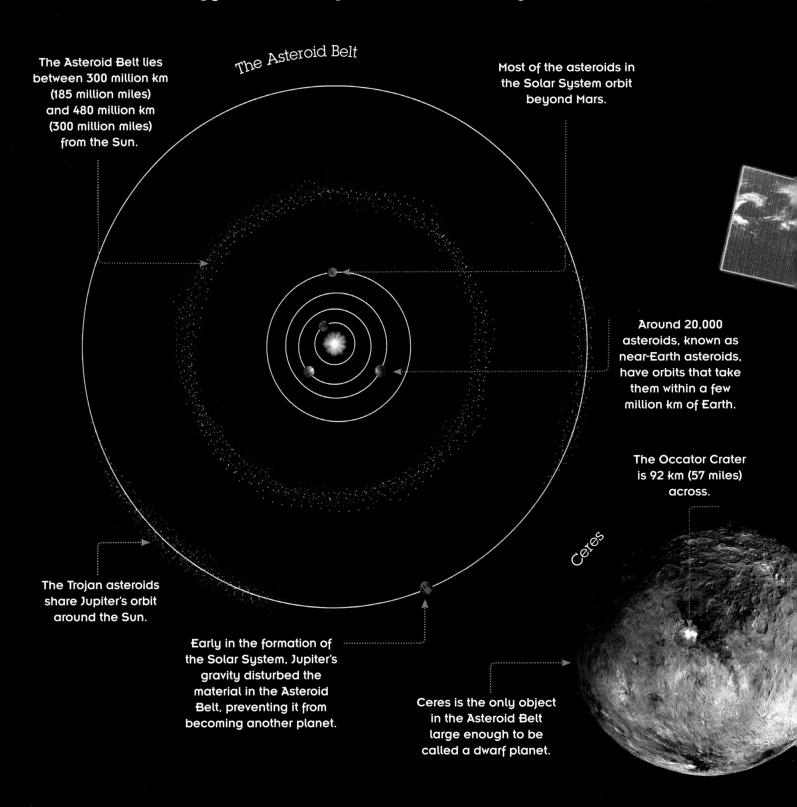

The Asteroid Belt

The Asteroid Belt lies between 300 million km (185 million miles) and 480 million km (300 million miles) from the Sun.

Most of the asteroids in the Solar System orbit beyond Mars.

Around 20,000 asteroids, known as near-Earth asteroids, have orbits that take them within a few million km of Earth.

The Occator Crater is 92 km (57 miles) across.

The Trojan asteroids share Jupiter's orbit around the Sun.

Ceres

Early in the formation of the Solar System, Jupiter's gravity disturbed the material in the Asteroid Belt, preventing it from becoming another planet.

Ceres is the only object in the Asteroid Belt large enough to be called a dwarf planet.

Named after the Roman goddess of the home, Vesta is around 525 km (326 miles) across.

Vesta

Gaspra was photographed by the *Galileo* probe in 1991.

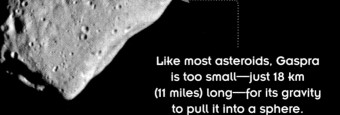

Gaspra

Like most asteroids, Gaspra is too small—just 18 km (11 miles) long—for its gravity to pull it into a sphere.

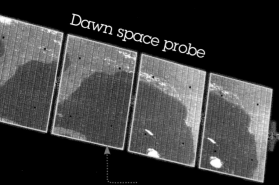

Dawn space probe

The high-gain antenna sends and receives information with Earth using radio waves.

The space probe was powered by solar panels, which absorb sunlight and convert it into electricity.

Dawn orbited Vesta and Ceres between 2011 and 2018.

Ceres

Type: Dwarf planet

Size: 940 km (580 miles) across

Mass: 0.00016 Earths

Moons: 0

Year: 4.6 Earth years

Day: 9 Earth hours

Surface Temperature: -163–-118°C (-261–-180°F)

Average Distance from the Sun: 413.8 million km (257 million miles)

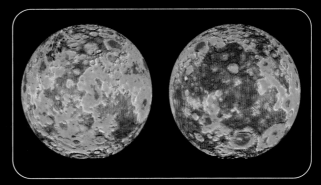

Created by *Dawn*, these maps of Ceres use blue (lowest), green, and red (highest) to show different land heights.

Chapter 2

OUTER SOLAR SYSTEM

The Outer Solar System is home to the four giant planets: Jupiter, Saturn, Uranus, and Neptune. The region stretches from Jupiter, around 778.5 million km (483.7 million miles) from the Sun, to where the Sun's influence finally starts to weaken, around 13.5 billion km (8.4 billion miles) from our star.

The four giant planets are made mostly of lighter materials than the smaller, rocky inner planets. The giant planets are large enough—and their gravity is strong enough—to stop light materials from drifting out into space.

Jupiter and Saturn are known as gas giants, because they are made largely of hydrogen and helium, which are gases at room temperature. Smaller than the gas giants, Uranus and Neptune are known as ice giants because they hold a lot of water, ammonia, and methane, which freeze into solid "ice" at much higher temperatures than hydrogen and helium.

However, none of the giant planets has a solid surface, since they are mostly swirling gases and liquids.

The Outer Solar System is also home to many smaller rocky or icy objects, including moons, asteroids, comets, and centaurs (see page 41). Beyond the orbit of Neptune are the Kuiper Belt and Scattered Disk, where there are at least 10 million objects, including some large enough to be called dwarf planets.

Jupiter, the largest planet in the Solar System, is 11 times the size of Earth.

Sun

Jupiter

Saturn

Uranus

Neptune

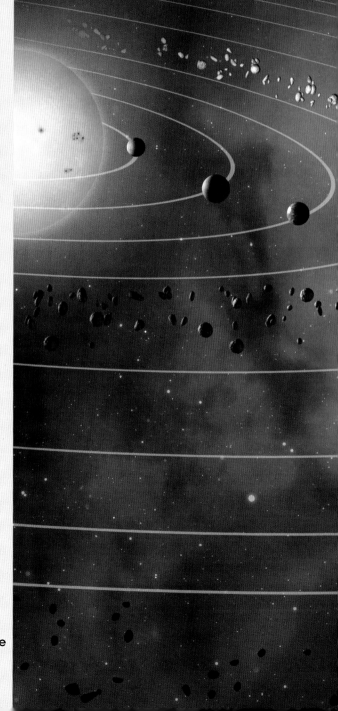

Discovering the Planets

Mercury, Venus, Mars, Jupiter, and Saturn can be seen without a telescope, so they were all watched by Babylonian astronomers more than 3,000 years ago. In 1781, William Herschel was the first to spot Uranus through his telescope. In 1846, Johann Gottfried Galle spotted Neptune after Urbain Le Verrier worked out its location by studying how Uranus was pulled by the gravity of a planet orbiting farther from the Sun.

◄········· Frenchman Urbain Le Verrier (1811–77) used mathematics to pinpoint the location of Neptune.

Far beyond the orbits of Mercury, Venus, Earth, and Mars are the four giant planets: Jupiter, Saturn, Uranus, and Neptune.

The Great Red Spot is seen in Jupiter's lower right quarter, to the south of the large white band known as the Equatorial Zone.

JUPITER

Jupiter is so large that its mass (or weight) is 2.5 times the mass of the other Solar System planets combined. The planet is made of similar materials to the Sun: mostly hydrogen, with some helium. Like the other giant planets, Jupiter has a ring system. The rings look fainter than Saturn's, as they are made of dust rather than shining ice.

Like Jupiter itself, the planet's atmosphere is mostly hydrogen and helium. Since Jupiter has no solid surface, there is no definite line where the atmosphere ends and the planet begins. Deep in the atmosphere, the hydrogen becomes so hot and so tightly squeezed by the pull of Jupiter's own gravity that it becomes a liquid ocean. Jupiter probably has a solid core made of iron and rock. The core may reach a temperature of 24,000°C (43,000°F).

The stripes and swirls seen in photographs of Jupiter are clouds, made of ammonia and water. Jupiter spins very quickly on its axis, making one rotation every 10 hours. This creates fast winds, often around 360 km (225 miles) per hour, which separate the clouds into dark and light horizontal bands.

Jupiter's winds also cause huge storms, which are regions of spinning gas and cloud. The largest storm is known as the Great Red Spot, which is currently over 16,000 km (9,900 miles) wide. Astronomers have been watching the storm since at least 1878.

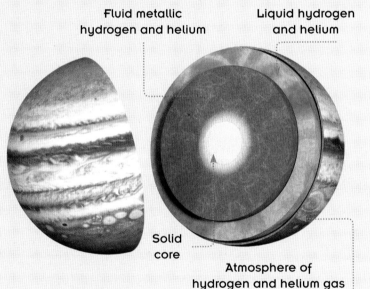

Fluid metallic hydrogen and helium

Liquid hydrogen and helium

Solid core

Atmosphere of hydrogen and helium gas

Jupiter has a layer of fluid metallic hydrogen and helium that is squeezed so tightly it behaves like a metal by conducting (or enabling the flow of) electricity.

Jupiter

Type: Gas giant planet

Size: 142,984 km (88,846 miles) across

Mass: 317.8 Earths

Moons: 79

Year: 11.86 Earth years

Day: 10 Earth hours

Surface Temperature: -108°C (-162°F)

Average Distance from the Sun: 778.5 million km (483.7 million miles)

Powered by three solar panels, the *Juno* space probe began to orbit Jupiter in 2016.

MOONS OF JUPITER

Jupiter has 79 known moons, orbiting the planet at between 128,000 km (80,000 miles) and 29 million km (18 million miles). The four largest moons, called the Galilean moons, were discovered by Italian astronomer Galileo Galilei (1564–1642) in 1610. While the Galilean moons are all over 3,000 km (1,860 miles) wide, the next largest moon is only 250 km (155 miles) across.

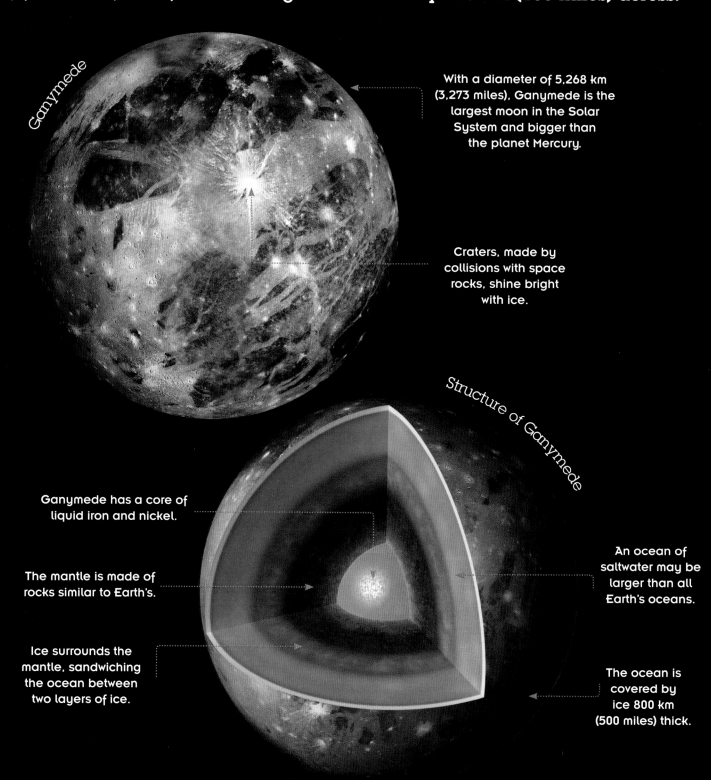

Ganymede

With a diameter of 5,268 km (3,273 miles), Ganymede is the largest moon in the Solar System and bigger than the planet Mercury.

Craters, made by collisions with space rocks, shine bright with ice.

Structure of Ganymede

Ganymede has a core of liquid iron and nickel.

The mantle is made of rocks similar to Earth's.

Ice surrounds the mantle, sandwiching the ocean between two layers of ice.

An ocean of saltwater may be larger than all Earth's oceans.

The ocean is covered by ice 800 km (500 miles) thick.

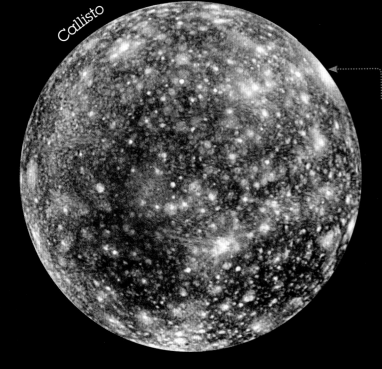

Callisto

Callisto is Jupiter's second largest moon and the third largest moon in the Solar System, after Saturn's moon Titan.

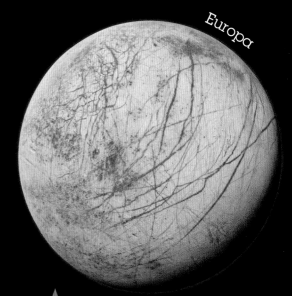

Europa

The third largest moon, Io has over 400 volcanoes, which spew lava over hundreds of kilometers.

Io

Beneath its frozen surface, Europa, the smallest of the Galilean moons, has an ocean that could possibly contain tiny life forms.

Io's volcanoes are caused by its rocks being squeezed, stretched, and melted by Jupiter's powerful gravity.

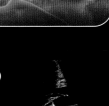

Io

Type: Moon

Size: 3,660 km (2,274 miles) across

Mass: 0.015 Earths

Year: 11.86 Earth years

Day: 10 Earth hours

Surface Temperature: -163°C (-262°F)

Average Distance from the Sun: 778.5 million km (483.7 million miles)

SATURN

The sixth planet from the Sun was named after the Roman god of wealth and farming. Saturn is the only planet in the Solar System which is less dense than water, meaning that its molecules are less tightly packed than those in water. If there were a bucket of water big enough to hold it, Saturn would float.

Saturn's structure is similar to Jupiter's, with a solid super-hot core of rock and metal surrounded by liquid hydrogen and helium, wrapped in an atmosphere of mostly hydrogen gas. Winds in Saturn's atmosphere can reach 1,800 km (1,000 miles) per hour, much faster than those of Jupiter. Yet storms are shorter than on the other gas giant. A storm known as the Great White Spot can be seen in Saturn's northern hemisphere for a few weeks once every Saturnian year (about every 29.46 Earth years), when this hemisphere tilts toward the Sun.

Saturn has 82 known moons, as well as countless moonlets, up to 500 m (1,640 ft) wide, that orbit in its rings. The planet's largest moon is Titan, which is 5,149 km (3,200 miles) across, a little larger than the planet Mercury.

While Saturn's swirling hydrogen cannot support living things, some of Saturn's moons are being studied for signs of life. Titan and Enceladus probably have oceans of water beneath an outer crust of ice. As in Earth's early oceans, it is possible that tiny life forms could develop in the water.

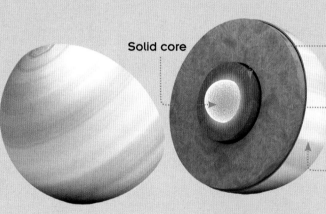

Solid core

Fluid metallic hydrogen and helium

Saturn's core is probably made of iron and nickel surrounded by rocky material.

Liquid hydrogen and helium

Atmosphere of hydrogen and helium gas

Saturn

Type: Gas giant planet

Size: 120,536 km (74,898 miles) across

Mass: 95.149 Earths

Moons: 82

Year: 29.46 Earth years

Day: 10.5 Earth hours

Surface Temperature: -139°C (-218°F)

Average Distance from the Sun: 1.4 billion km (890 million miles)

The *Cassini* space probe created these six images of Saturn's moon Titan using infrared cameras, which are able to "see" through the moon's hazy atmosphere (middle).

Saturn's second largest moon, Rhea, orbits the planet once every 4.5 Earth days.

SATURN'S RINGS

Saturn has the Solar System's largest ring system. The rings are billions of chunks of ice and rock which orbit the planet between around 7,000 km (4,350 miles) and 400,000 km (248,550 miles) away. The chunks range from tiny grains to a few hundred meters wide.

In 1610, astronomer Galileo Galilei was the first to glimpse Saturn's rings, blurrily, through his telescope. The main, brightest rings were named with a letter, working alphabetically in the order they were discovered. Each ring orbits the planet at a different speed. There are many gaps within and between the rings, largely caused by the pulls of Saturn's moons. The largest gap, 4,800 km (2,980 miles) wide, is called the Cassini Division. Although the rings are thousands of kilometers wide, they are only between 10 m (33 ft) and 1 km (0.6 miles) thick.

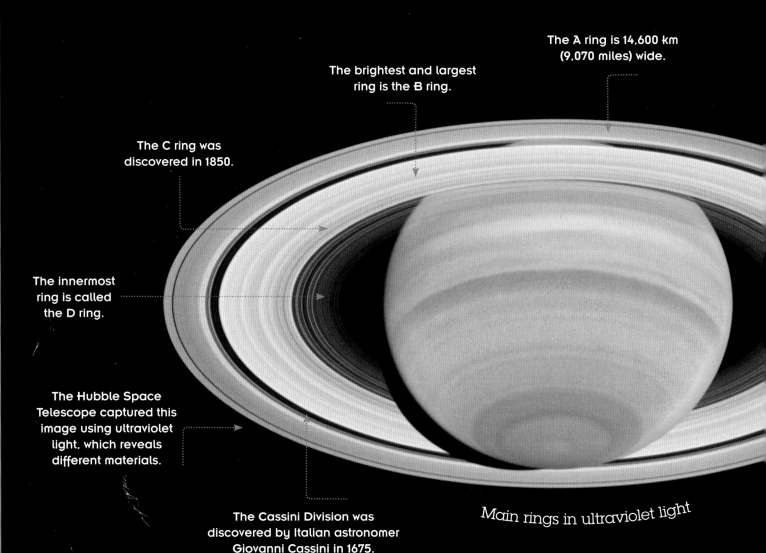

The A ring is 14,600 km (9,070 miles) wide.

The brightest and largest ring is the B ring.

The C ring was discovered in 1850.

The innermost ring is called the D ring.

The Hubble Space Telescope captured this image using ultraviolet light, which reveals different materials.

The Cassini Division was discovered by Italian astronomer Giovanni Cassini in 1675.

Main rings in ultraviolet light

Saturn's rings may have formed quite recently, between 10 million and 100 million years ago. They are possibly the remains of a moon that was struck by a comet or asteroid. Another theory is that the chunks were formed when comets and asteroids were torn to pieces by Saturn's gravity.

Formation of the rings

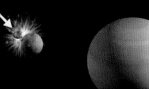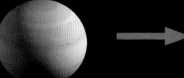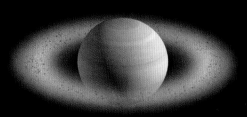

1. One of Saturn's moons is shattered by an asteroid.

2. The rubble spreads into a cloud but is held close to Saturn by its gravity.

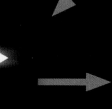

3. The jumbled fragments crash into each other, falling into a more circular orbit around Saturn's equator.

4. The pulls of Saturn's moons create gaps in the rings.

5. A circular, flat ring system is formed.

Taken by the Hubble Space Telescope, this brightened photograph shows Uranus, its inner rings, and five of its moons, including Ariel at bottom right.

URANUS

Uranus is made mostly of hot, flowing water, ammonia, and methane, which surrounds a rocky core. The planet's thick atmosphere contains hydrogen, helium, and methane gas. The methane makes Uranus look blue-ish through a telescope, as it absorbs red light, leaving light that our eyes see as blue.

Uranus's great distance from the Sun means it takes 84 Earth years to complete one orbit. Like all the planets, as Uranus travels round the Sun it also rotates round its own axis, taking 17 hours to make one rotation. Yet, unlike the other planets, Uranus's axis is tilted sideways. The planet rotates on its side, with its ring system pointing "upward." When one pole of Uranus is tilted to the Sun, it has 42 Earth years of light, followed by 42 years of darkness when it is tilted away. Astronomers think Uranus's sideways tilt may be the result of a collision with an Earth-sized planet soon after its formation.

Uranus has 13 dark rings that are difficult to see through a telescope. They are made of ice, dust, and a dark material that astronomers cannot yet identify. The planet has 27 known moons, orbiting within and beyond the rings. Most of them are named after characters from the plays of William Shakespeare. The two largest, Titania and Oberon, are named after the queen and king of the fairies in *A Midsummer Night's Dream*.

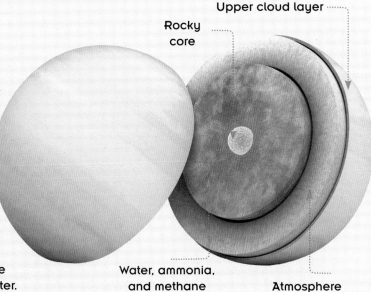

Rocky core

Upper cloud layer

Water, ammonia, and methane

Atmosphere

Although Uranus is known as an ice giant, it is made mostly of hot, swirling materials rather than frozen water.

Uranus

Type: Ice giant planet

Size: 51,118 km (31,763 miles) across

Mass: 14.536 Earths

Moons: 27

Year: 84 Earth years

Day: 17 Earth hours

Surface Temperature: -197°C (-323°F)

Average Distance from the Sun: 2.9 billion km (1.8 billion miles)

The space probe *Voyager 2* took this photograph of Uranus's moon Titania, which is 1,578 km (981 miles) across.

NEPTUNE

The eighth planet from the Sun, Neptune can never be seen without a telescope. The planet was named after the Roman god of the sea. It is made of similar materials to its fellow ice giant, Uranus. Despite being slightly smaller than Uranus, Neptune has a greater mass.

When the space probe *Voyager 2* passed Neptune in 1989, it beamed back to Earth the first detailed photos of the planet. One feature revealed by the probe was the Great Dark Spot, a storm similar to Jupiter's Great Red Spot. The storm's darkness was created by a hole in the planet's blue clouds of methane. Around 13,000 km (8,000 miles) across, the storm had winds up to 2,100 km (1,300 miles) per hour, the fastest recorded in the Solar System. When the planet was next photographed in detail, by the Hubble Space Telescope in 1994, the storm had disappeared. Similar storms have appeared since, seeming to fade within a few months.

Neptune has 14 known moons. The largest, Triton, is 2,710 km (1,680 miles) across, making it the seventh largest moon in the Solar System, after four moons of Jupiter, one of Saturn, and Earth's Moon. Unlike the Solar System's other large moons, Triton orbits its planet in the opposite direction from the way Neptune is turning. This suggests that the moon did not form at the same time and place as its planet. Triton may have been a dwarf planet orbiting in the Kuiper Belt, but was drawn in by Neptune's gravity.

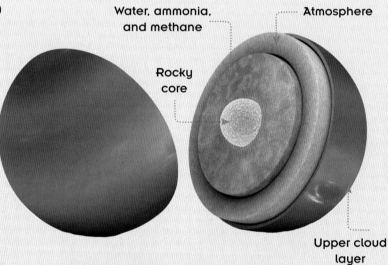

Water, ammonia, and methane

Atmosphere

Rocky core

Upper cloud layer

The temperature of Neptune's core may be around 5,100°C (9,200°F).

Neptune

Type: Ice giant planet

Size: 49,528 km (30,775 miles) across

Mass: 17.147 Earths

Moons: 14

Year: 165 Earth years

Day: 16 Earth hours

Surface Temperature: -201°C (-330°F)

Average Distance from the Sun: 4.5 billion km (2.8 billion miles)

This illustration shows Neptune's tiny moon Hippocamp (in the foreground), which may have broken off a larger moon, Proteus (in the background).

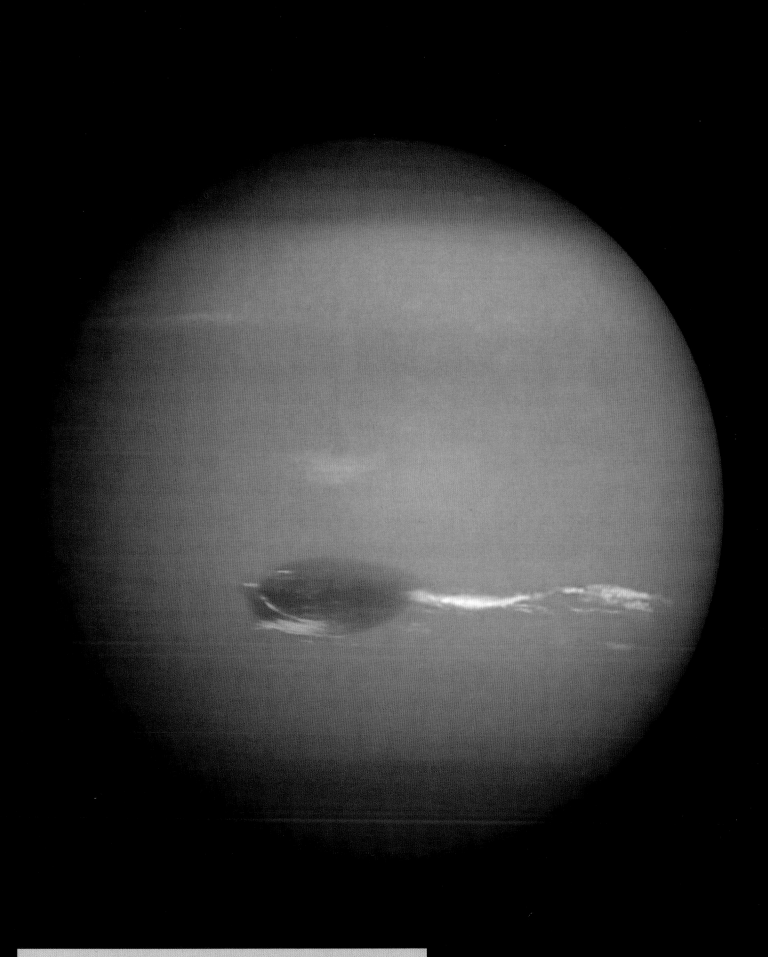

Voyager 2, the only spacecraft that has visited the ice giants, photographed Neptune's Great Dark Spot in 1989.

This illustration imagines the Kuiper Belt, where icy objects orbit at distances of up to 7.5 billion km (4.7 billion miles) from the Sun.

THE KUIPER BELT

Beyond Neptune is the Kuiper Belt, a ring of objects left over from the formation of the Solar System. If these objects had not been stirred by Neptune's gravity, they might have pulled together into a planet. The smallest objects spotted so far are 1 km (0.6 miles) across, while the largest are big enough to be called dwarf planets (see page 42).

The Kuiper Belt is named after astronomer Gerard Kuiper (1905–73), who suggested in 1951 that there were undiscovered icy bodies in the Outer Solar System. The first Kuiper Belt Object (KBO) was spotted through a telescope at Hawaii's Mauna Kea Observatories in 1992. The Kuiper Belt stretches for around 3 billion km (1.86 billion miles) beyond the orbit of Neptune.

Unlike the asteroids in the Inner Solar System's Asteroid Belt, which are made of rock and metal, KBOs are made of rock and frozen ammonia, methane, and water. Most KBOs have roughly circular orbits. The Kuiper Belt may be the original home of objects called centaurs. These rocky and icy objects were possibly disturbed from the Kuiper Belt by Neptune's gravity, giving them orbits that cross the paths of the giant planets until they are thrown aside or destroyed.

Overlapping with the Kuiper Belt and stretching further from the Sun is the Scattered Disk. This region contains objects that have been scattered yet more by Neptune's gravity. The objects have orbits that are greatly stretched rather than circular, journeying above and below the flat plane in which the planets orbit.

In 2015–19, the *New Horizons* space probe did flybys of KBOs Pluto and Arrokoth.

Arrokoth

Type: Kuiper Belt Object

Size: 36 km (22 miles) across

Mass: Unknown

Moons: 0

Year: 297.7 Earth years

Day: Unknown

Surface Temperature: -244– -213°C (-407– -415°F)

Average Distance from the Sun: 6.7 billion km (4.2 billion miles)

Arrokoth probably formed when two objects joined together.

BEYOND THE KUIPER BELT

The Kuiper Belt stretches 7.5 billion km (4.7 billion miles) from the Sun, but this is far from the edge of the Solar System. We can say the Solar System ends 13.5 billion km (8.4 billion miles) from the Sun, at the edge of a bubble-like region of space called the heliosphere. Or we could say that it ends where the pull of the Sun's gravity is no stronger than the pull of other stars, which is more than 1,000 times farther away.

The solar wind is a stream of energized particles that flow from the Sun at around 400 km (250 miles) per second. The wind fills a bubble called the heliosphere. At the edge of the heliosphere, the heliopause is the point where the pressure from the solar wind is equal to the pressure of wind coming from space.

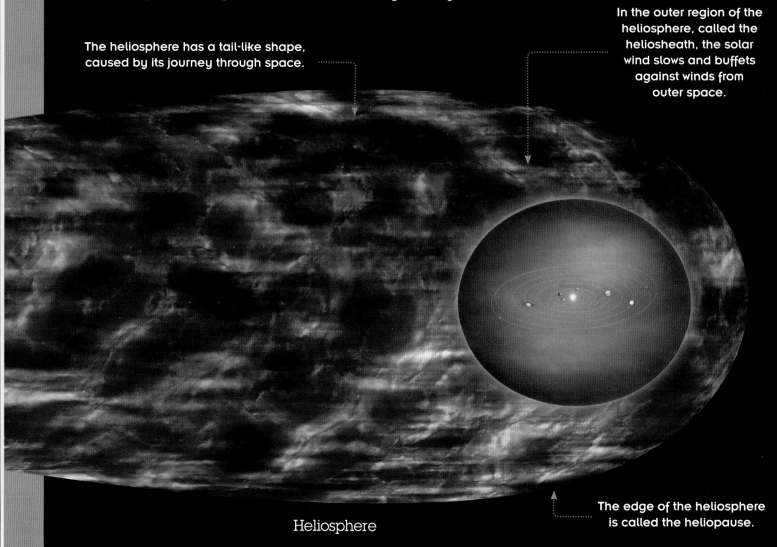

In the outer region of the heliosphere, called the heliosheath, the solar wind slows and buffets against winds from outer space.

The heliosphere has a tail-like shape, caused by its journey through space.

Heliosphere

The edge of the heliosphere is called the heliopause.

Within around 18.7 trillion km (11.6 trillion miles) from the Sun, the pull of its gravity is stronger than the pull of nearby stars. Astronomers predict that more distant large objects will one day be found in this vast outer region, although they do not yet have proof of their existence. Some think that a ninth planet may be orbiting here. Most believe the region holds the Oort Cloud, containing trillions of icy objects. The Oort Cloud was the original home of most comets, small icy objects that have elliptical orbits through the Solar System. These comets were set in motion toward the Sun when stirred by the gravity of passing stars.

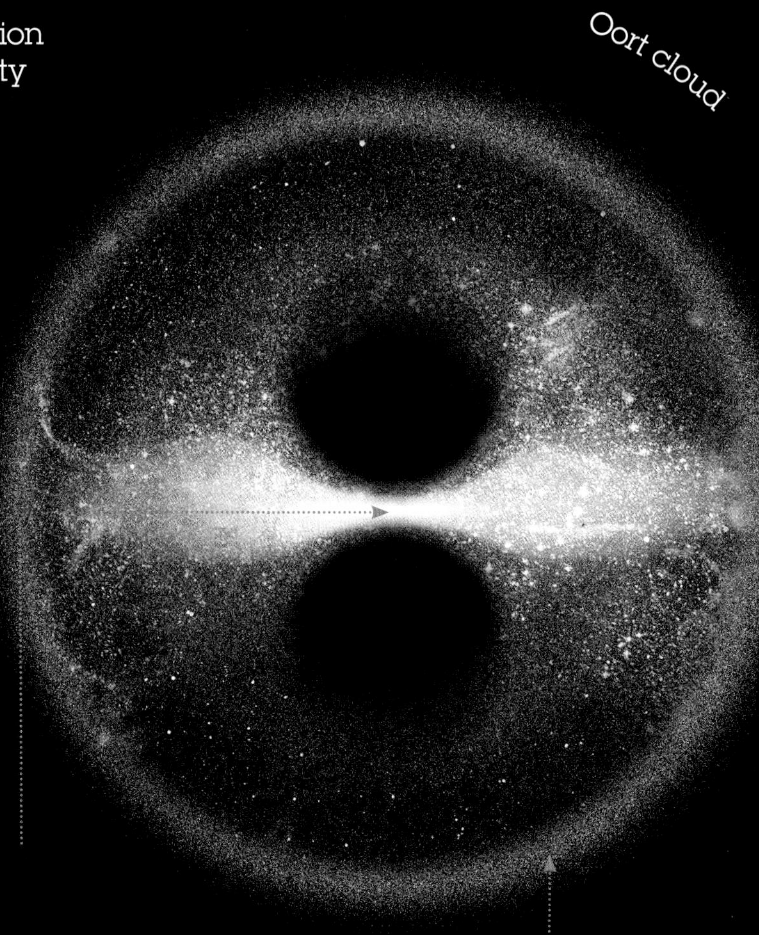

The Sun and planets are too small to be seen at this scale.

Oort cloud

The Oort Cloud has a pancake-shaped inner cloud and a ball-shaped outer cloud of objects.

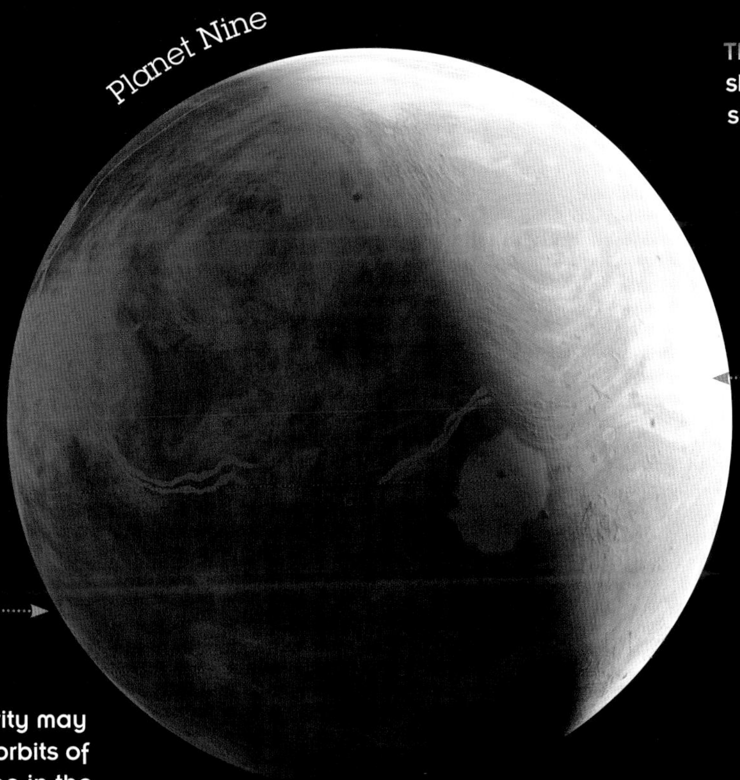

Planet Nine

If Planet Nine exists, it probably orbits 60–120 billion km (37–75 billion miles) from the Sun.

The planet's gravity may be affecting the orbits of objects we can see in the far Solar System.

Chapter 3

STARS

Most of the glowing dots we see in the night sky are stars. Apart from the Sun, our nearest star, they are all trillions of kilometers away. Astronomers think there may be 1 septillion (1 followed by 24 zeros) stars in the Universe, most of them too distant to be seen by the naked eye.

Stars are glowing balls of gas, mostly hydrogen and helium. The gas has got so hot that it has become plasma. Like everything else, plasma is made of tiny atoms. In a plasma, the atoms are so hot that particles called electrons break away from them. Each electron carries a tiny electric charge, which gives plasma an electric charge.

A star is hot and glowing because hydrogen atoms are constantly crashing together in its core. These collisions create helium atoms and release energy in the form of light and heat. All stars eventually run out of hydrogen. Without this fuel, they begin to change—and finally die.

A star is held together by its own gravity, a force that pulls all objects—from atoms to galaxies—toward each other. A star's gravity may also hold other objects in orbit around it. Our Sun keeps all the objects in the Solar System spinning around it. Our star is far from the only star with orbiting planets. Astronomers estimate there are billions of other solar systems in the Universe.

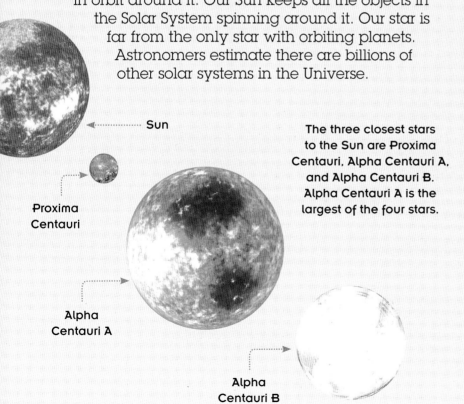

Sun

Proxima
Centauri

Alpha
Centauri A

Alpha
Centauri B

The three closest stars to the Sun are Proxima Centauri, Alpha Centauri A, and Alpha Centauri B. Alpha Centauri A is the largest of the four stars.

Star Spectrum

The light that human eyes can see is made up of all shades of the rainbow, known as the spectrum. If a star is very hot, its light is bluer. If it is cooler, its light looks redder. The astronomer Annie Jump Cannon helped develop our system of classifying stars by their temperature and shade.

Annie Jump Cannon (1863–1941) put stars into classes O, B, A, F, G, K, and M, with O the hottest.

The light from star V838 Monocerotis (glowing red) is reflecting off clouds of gas and dust in this photograph by the Hubble Space Telescope.

STAR TYPES

The heavier a star is, the hotter and brighter it is. The lightest stars are red and relatively dim. Medium stars are yellow, while the heaviest are often blue and very bright. Smaller stars are usually called dwarfs, while large stars are known as giants or supergiants.

For most of its life, a star is in the "main sequence." This is the period when it is turning hydrogen into helium in its core. There is a balance between gravity trying to shrink it and heat making it grow bigger. A star will remain in this stable, main sequence stage of its life until it runs out of hydrogen. Most main sequence stars are known as dwarf stars.

Red dwarf

Red dwarfs, such as Proxima Centauri, are the smallest and coolest main sequence stars.

Blue supergiant

Yellow dwarfs, like our Sun, are medium-sized main sequence stars around 1 or 2 million km (0.6–1.2 million miles) across.

 Yellow dwarf

Blue supergiants, such as Rigel in the Orion constellation, are very bright.

The heavier the star, the faster it uses up its store of hydrogen. The largest stars may last for only a few million years, while the smallest might survive for 10 trillion years, which is many times longer than the 13.8 billion years the Universe has existed. When the larger main sequence stars have run out of hydrogen, they swell into a red giant or a supergiant. Smaller main sequence stars shrink into a white dwarf, around one-hundredth the size of the Sun.

A supergiant can swap between blue and red phases as it shrinks and grows.

A red giant forms when a medium-sized star, like the Sun, has run out of hydrogen in its core and starts to expand as hydrogen is used up farther out.

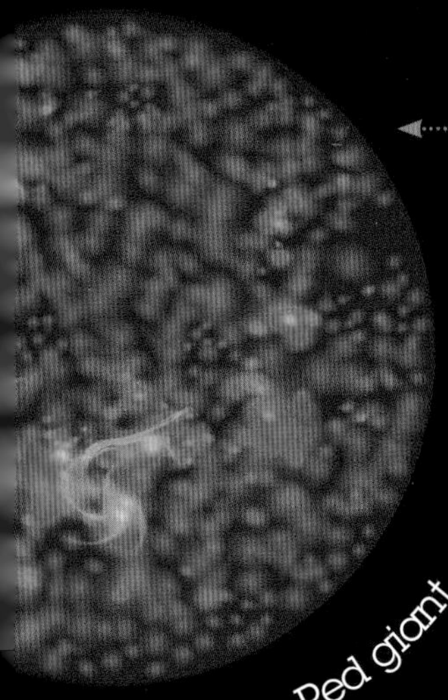

Red giants, such as Aldebaran in the Taurus constellation, range from 100 million km (60 million miles) to 1 billion km (600 million miles) across.

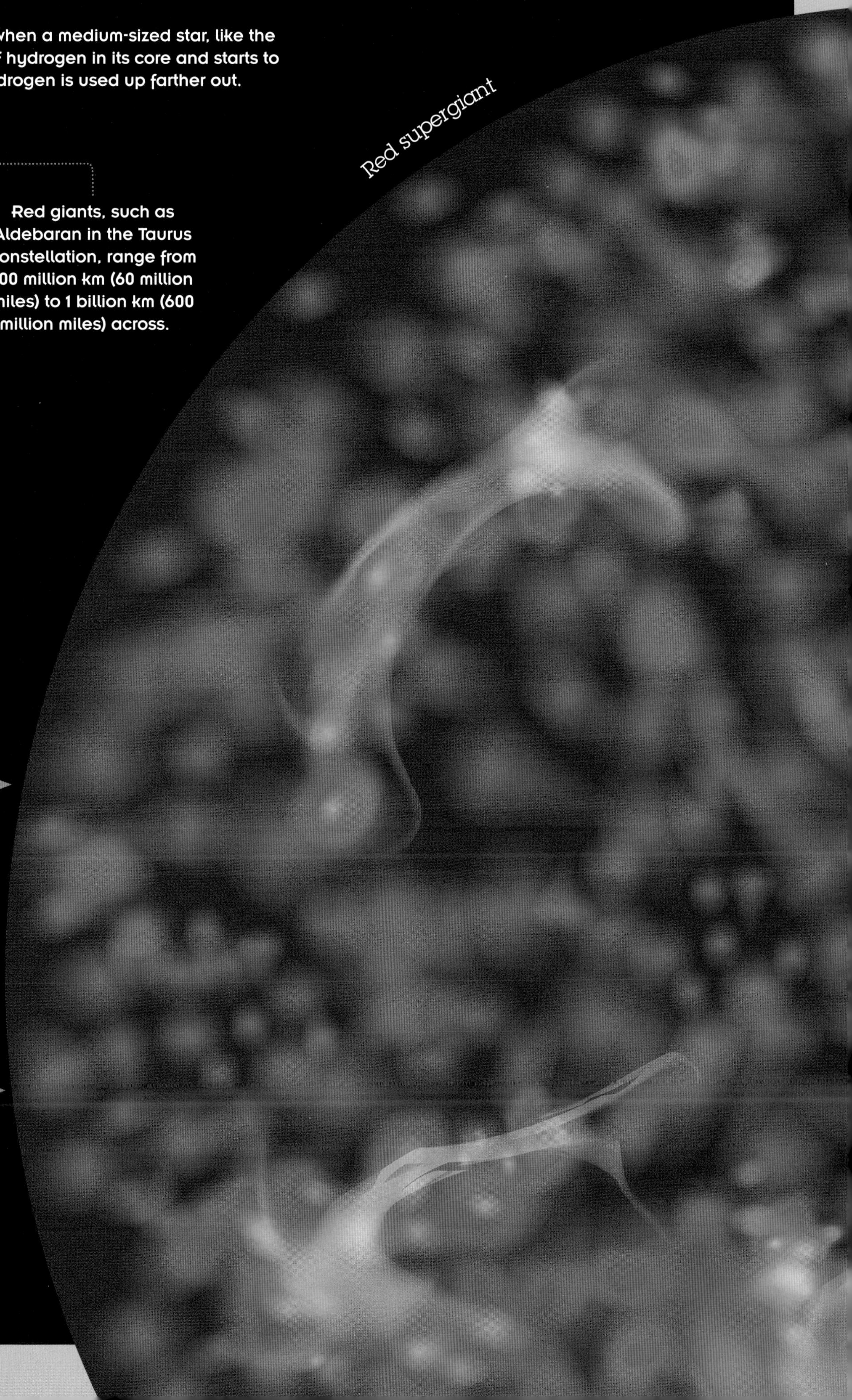

Red giant

Red supergiant

A red supergiant forms when a star between 8 and 30 times the mass of the Sun runs out of hydrogen.

Red supergiants, such as Betelgeuse in the Orion constellation, are the largest but not the brightest stars.

The Sun's brightness can blind human eyes, but the cameras of the Solar Dynamics Observatory take photographs that enable us to see its features.

THE SUN

The Sun is a medium-sized, yellow dwarf star, although its light is white rather than yellow. Our star formed around 4.57 billion years ago and is likely to survive another 5 billion years. The Sun's heat and light enable life to flourish on Earth. Without the Sun, plants could not grow and animals would not find food.

In the Sun's core, hydrogen atoms are constantly fusing into helium. This releases energy, which travels outward to the Sun's surface. First, it travels through the radiative zone, moving by a process called radiation: the energy is carried by tiny particles, called photons. After about 170,000 years, the energy reaches the convection zone. Here, bubbles of hot plasma carry the energy by convection: They rise to the surface like hot water in a pan.

The surface of the Sun is called the photosphere. It gives off the energy we see as sunlight and feel as heat, which reaches Earth about 8 minutes later. Above the photosphere is the Sun's atmosphere, which astronomers divide into the chromosphere and the outer corona.

When the Sun runs out of hydrogen in its core, in around 5 billion years, its outer layers will expand, transforming the Sun into a red giant. This process will swallow Mercury and Venus—and fry Earth. The Sun will spend half a billion years as a red giant, while it uses its helium atoms as fuel. Eventually, when the helium is gone, the Sun will shed its outer layers and become a white dwarf. Slowly, over billions or trillions of years, it will cool down.

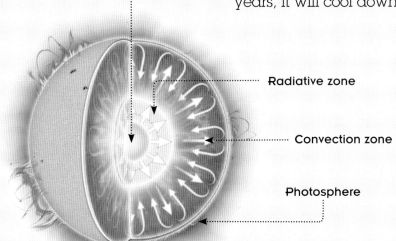

Core

Radiative zone

Convection zone

Photosphere

The Sun's core reaches around 15 million °C (27 million °F).

The Sun

Type: Yellow dwarf star

Size: 1.39 million km (0.86 million miles) across

Mass: 333,000 Earths

Age: 4.57 billion years

Surface Temperature: 5,500°C (10,000°F)

Distance from Milky Way Core: 27,200 light years

The Sun is surrounded by a halo, or ring, when its light is reflected and bent by ice crystals in Earth's atmosphere.

SOLAR ACTIVITY

With dark sunspots and sudden explosions of energy called flares, the Sun's surface is extremely active. This solar activity is caused by magnetism, a force created by the movement of electric charges. The amount of solar activity changes through an 11-year period known as the solar cycle.

Every substance is made of atoms. Each atom has particles called electrons circling its nucleus, or core. Electrons carry electric charges. Their movement creates an electric current, making each electron behave like a tiny magnet. A magnet attracts or repels other magnets. In a star's plasma, the electrons have been completely separated from their atoms, creating areas of powerful magnetic forces called magnetic fields. Since the plasma is constantly moving, the magnetic fields twist and tangle. This creates activity on the Sun's surface.

The Sun's magnetic field

The Sun's magnetic field has two poles, like a bar magnet.

The Sun has a north and a south magnetic pole. A pole is the location on a star or planet where its magnetic field lines are vertical, either pointing downward (the North Pole) or upward (the South Pole). Every 11 years, the Sun's north and south poles swap places. This swap happens when solar activity is busiest. At these times, intense flares and bursts of charged particles can damage Earth's radio communications and electricity supplies.

Solar flare

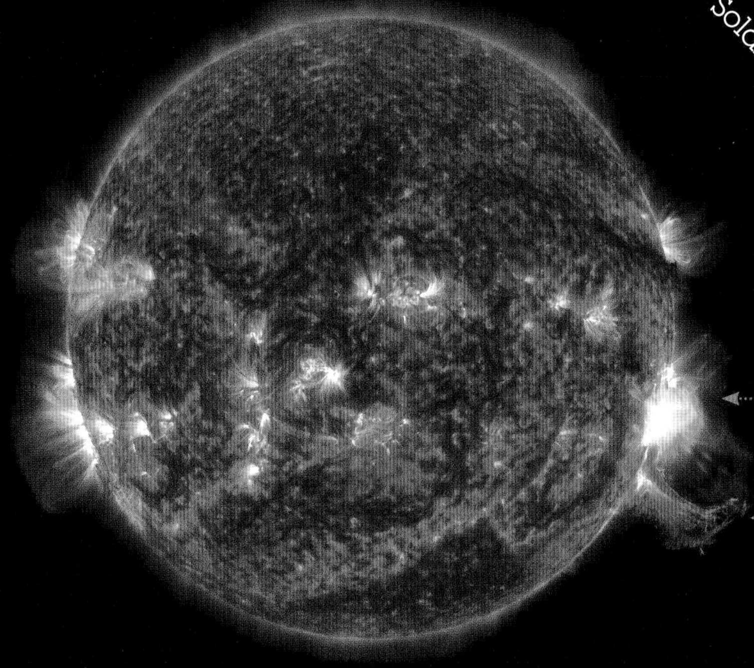

A solar flare is a burst of light, heat, and other energy caused by the tangling of magnetic field lines.

Material from the Sun erupts into space.

Sunspots

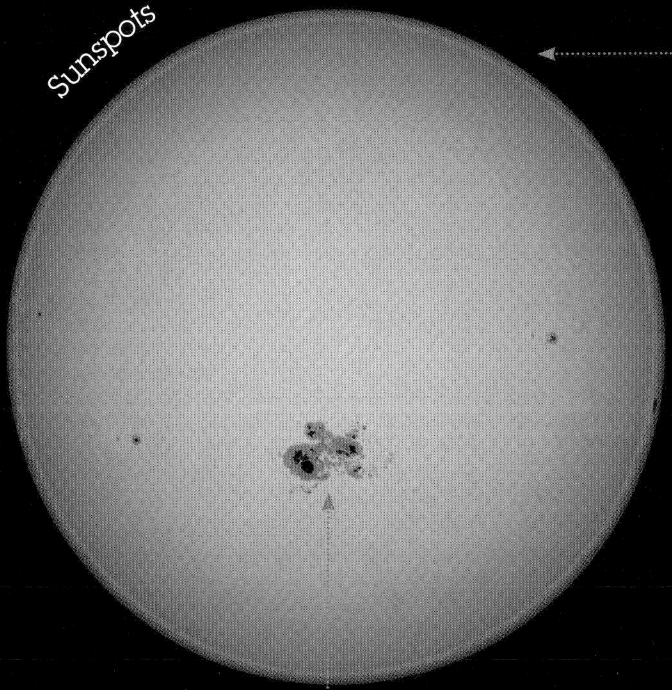

This image from the Solar Dynamics Observatory is created from "ordinary" photographs and information about magnetic activity.

Coronal loop

Sunspots, which appear and disappear, are cooler areas caused by magnetic field lines stopping hot plasma from rising to the surface.

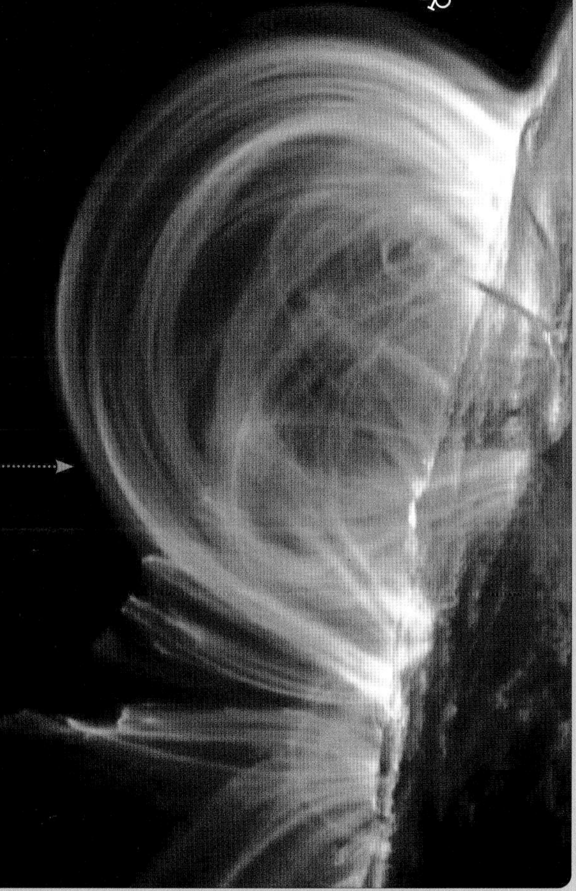

A coronal loop can be seen when a loop of magnetic field traps glowing plasma.

The darker areas in the Pillars of Creation are clumps where new stars are forming.

THE PILLARS OF CREATION

Around 5,700 light years from Earth is a cloud of dust and gas called the Eagle Nebula. The nebula (from the Latin for "cloud") is home to stellar nurseries, including the Pillars of Creation, thick areas of cloud where new stars are born. The process of star formation takes 100 million years. Across the Universe, about 400 million stars are born every day.

A new star forms in a thick cloud of dust and hydrogen and helium gas. A clump starts to grow in the cloud, perhaps caused by a collision with another cloud or the wind from a nearby star. As the clump grows, its gravity pulls more dust and gas into a ball. Eventually, the ball gets so big that it collapses in on itself. The collapse makes the material at the heart of the ball heat up. When it reaches 15 million °C (27 million °F), hydrogen atoms start to join together to form helium atoms. This releases an immense amount of energy. The new star is now born, shining with the light of all the energy it releases.

The Pillars of Creation are thick clouds shaped like elephants' trunks. Tall pillars such as these often form at the edges of nebulae. The tallest pillar is 5 light years long, much larger than our Solar System. Hidden inside the pillars are newborn and forming stars. The energy of all its bright young stars makes the gases in the Eagle Nebula glow. This makes it an emission nebula, since it emits (or gives off) light.

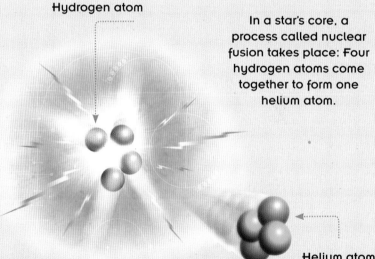

Hydrogen atom

In a star's core, a process called nuclear fusion takes place: Four hydrogen atoms come together to form one helium atom.

Helium atom

The Eagle Nebula

Type: Emission nebula

Size: 70 light years across

Mass: 12,000 Suns

Age: 1–2 million years

Average Temperature: -270°C (-450°F)

Distance from the Sun: 5,700 light years

Energy from newborn stars makes the Eagle Nebula's hydrogen gas glow red. The Pillars of Creation are near the middle of the photograph.

THE SEVEN SISTERS

The Seven Sisters, also known as the Pleiades, is an open star cluster, a group of stars that formed from the same cloud and are around the same age. The stars are held loosely together by the pulls of their gravity, but they will eventually be dragged apart. The cluster contains around 1,000 stars, but only 14 can be seen by the naked eye from Earth.

The stars in the Seven Sisters probably formed around 115 million years ago. The stars that can be seen easily from Earth are bright, very hot, and blue. Most of the cluster's other stars are fainter and red. The cluster also contains many brown dwarfs, star-like objects that are too small for hydrogen atoms to start fusing in their core.

The Seven Sisters cluster will stay together for around another 250 million years, when it will have been pulled apart by the gravity of other stars or nebulae. In contrast, globular star clusters stay together for billions of years. Globular clusters contain many more stars, are more sphere-like in shape, and are much more tightly bound by gravity than open clusters.

The Seven Sisters gets its name from its nine brightest stars, which are named after seven sisters from Greek mythology and their parents, Atlas and Pleione. According to the myths, the god Atlas was forced to carry the sky on his shoulders. To comfort him, the king of the gods, Zeus, turned his daughters into stars to keep him company.

The Seven Sisters can be seen in the constellation of Taurus, the bull, shown here in a 19th-century star chart.

The Seven Sisters

Type: Open cluster

Size: 16 light years across

Mass: 800 Suns

Age: 115 million years

Surface Temperature of Brightest Star: 12,000°C (21,600°F)

Distance from the Sun: 445 light years

In this infrared image of the Seven Sisters, the thickest clouds of dust are shown in yellow and red, while thinner dust is green.

The brightest star in the Seven Sisters is Alcyone (in the middle), which is 10 times the size of the Sun.

STAR SYSTEMS

A star system is a small group of stars that orbit each other. A star system is much smaller than a star cluster or a galaxy, which contain hundreds to trillions of stars. Most star systems contain two stars, called binary systems, or three stars, called triple systems, but groups of up to nine have been found.

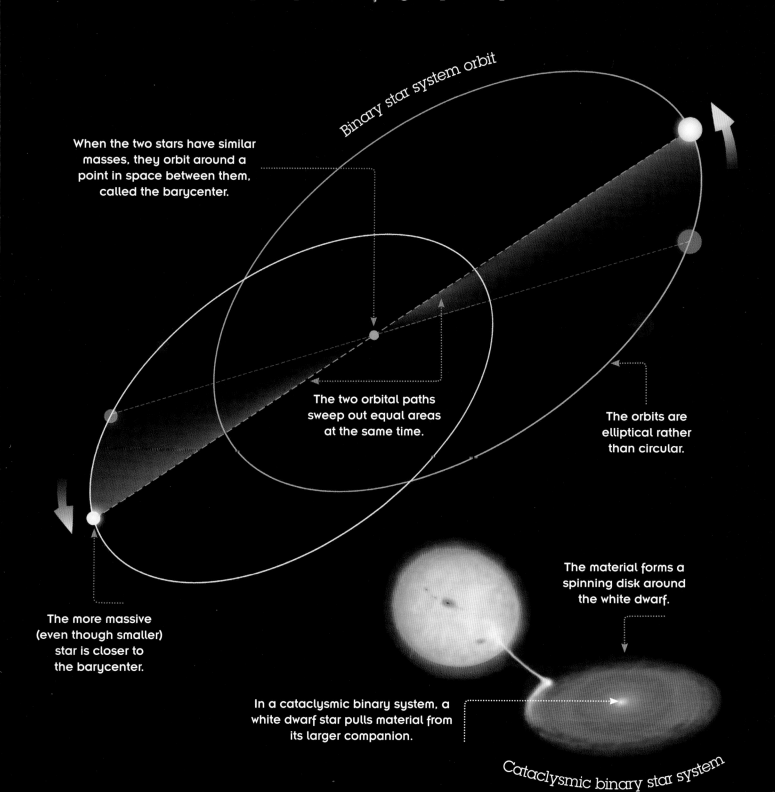

Binary star system orbit

When the two stars have similar masses, they orbit around a point in space between them, called the barycenter.

The two orbital paths sweep out equal areas at the same time.

The orbits are elliptical rather than circular.

The more massive (even though smaller) star is closer to the barycenter.

The material forms a spinning disk around the white dwarf.

In a cataclysmic binary system, a white dwarf star pulls material from its larger companion.

Cataclysmic binary star system

This Hubble Space Telescope photograph shows the binary system of Sirius A and Sirius B, which orbit each other every 50 years.

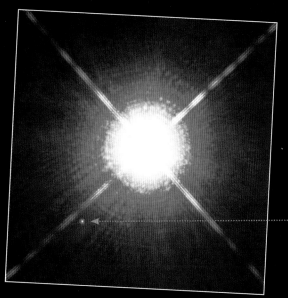

Sirius A and Sirius B binary star system

Sirius B is a small white dwarf, lying around 3 billion km (1.9 billion miles) from its larger partner.

In this illustration, our Sun is surrounded by the Oort Cloud ring of objects.

Alpha Centauri triple star system

Proxima Centauri, the nearest star to the Sun, makes one orbit of Alpha Centauri A and B every 555,000 years.

Alpha Centauri A and Alpha Centauri B orbit each other once every 80 years.

Sirius A

Type: Blue-white dwarf star

Size: 2.38 million km (1.48 million miles) across

Mass: 2 Suns

Age: 250 million years

Surface Temperature: 9,700°C (17,500°F)

Distance from the Sun: 8.6 light years

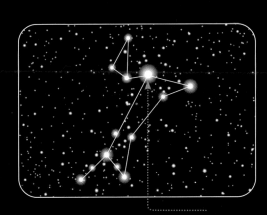

The Sirius system, in the constellation of Canis Major, is the brightest "star" in the night sky.

A white dwarf star can be seen at the heart of the nebula, the surrounding bubble and feathery streaks formed by gases as they are blown away.

THE CLOWN FACE NEBULA

The Clown Face Nebula is a glowing cloud of gas and dust. It is known as a planetary nebula, but it was not formed by a planet. The cloud was thrown out by a dying red giant star. The Clown Face Nebula is one of around 3,000 planetary nebulae in our Milky Way Galaxy.

All planetary nebulae are formed by red giant stars. Only medium-sized stars, between around 0.3 and 8 times the mass of our Sun, become red giants when they run out of hydrogen fuel. Smaller stars shrink straight into a white dwarf, while larger stars explode as a supernova (see page 62). Toward the end of its life, our Sun will form a planetary nebula.

When a Sun-like star runs out of hydrogen, its outer layers expand, turning it into a red giant. Yet the star's core shrinks and heats up,

until it is hot enough for helium atoms to start fusing into carbon and oxygen atoms. This releases huge amounts of energy, throwing the star's atmosphere out into space.

The gases form a cloud around the dying star, which gives off light, making the gases glow. This planetary nebula will last for only around 10,000 years, before the gases drift away. At the same time, the star is running out of helium. Without fuel, the remains of the star, known as a white dwarf, slowly cools and fades over trillions of years.

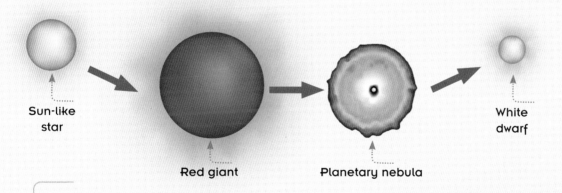

Sun-like star

Red giant

Planetary nebula

White dwarf

Sun-like stars spend a few million years as a red giant before creating a planetary nebula.

The Clown Face Nebula

Type: Planetary nebula

Size: 0.7 light years across

Mass: 0.3 Suns

Age: 10,000 years

Temperature of Gas: 10,000°C (18,000°F)

Distance from the Sun: 5,000 light years

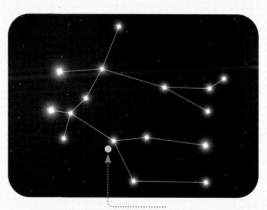

The Clown Face nebula can be seen with a small telescope in the constellation of Gemini.

THE CRAB NEBULA

This nebula was left behind by a massive explosion, called a supernova, which was seen by Chinese astronomers in 1054. The supernova took place when a huge star, perhaps 10 times the mass of our Sun, reached the end of its life. The explosion created a neutron star and cloud of glowing gas and dust.

After a massive star runs out of fuel, its core collapses, releasing extraordinary amounts of energy in a supernova explosion. A supernova gives off as much light as an entire galaxy of stars, before fading over a few weeks or months.

The explosion throws out an expanding cloud of gas and dust, called a supernova remnant. The gas in the Crab Nebula is still expanding by 1,500 km (930 miles) per second. Astronomers know of 270 supernova remnants in our galaxy, although many more are probably hidden by dust.

A supernova leaves behind a neutron star or, in the case of the most massive stars, a black hole (see page 64). A neutron star is only 20 km (12 miles) across but has a mass equal to our Sun. Some neutron stars spin very fast, up to 716 times per second, and give out powerful beams of energy. This has earned them the name pulsars, as their light appears to pulse as they turn. The neutron star at the heart of the Crab Nebula is a pulsar.

Massive stars end their life as a neutron star or black hole.

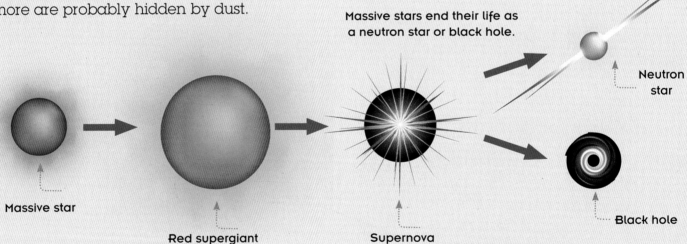

Massive star

Red supergiant

Supernova

Neutron star

Black hole

The Crab Nebula

Type: Supernova remnant

Size: 11 light years across

Mass: 2–3 Suns

Age: 1,000 years

Temperature of Gas: 15,000°C (27,000°F)

Distance from the Sun: 6,500 light years

This illustration imagines the neutron star, known as the Crab Pulsar, at the heart of the Crab Nebula.

This image was created by five different telescopes, showing five types of energy given off by the Crab Nebula: radio waves (red), X-rays (purple), infrared (yellow), ultraviolet (blue), and visible light (green).

BLACK HOLES

A black hole is a region of space where gravity is so strong that nothing can escape its pull. If anything—a star, planet, or light itself—crosses a boundary around a black hole, called an event horizon, it will be sucked inside. Black holes can form when an extremely massive star collapses in a supernova.

The larger an object's mass, the greater the pull of its gravity. If enough mass is squeezed into a small enough space, its gravity can deform space—creating a black hole. This can happen when a star more than 20 times the mass of the Sun runs out of fuel and collapses in on itself. Such black holes, known as stellar black holes, have a mass from 5 to 100 times our Sun's. Once a black hole has formed, it can grow by sucking in surrounding gas, dust, and stars.

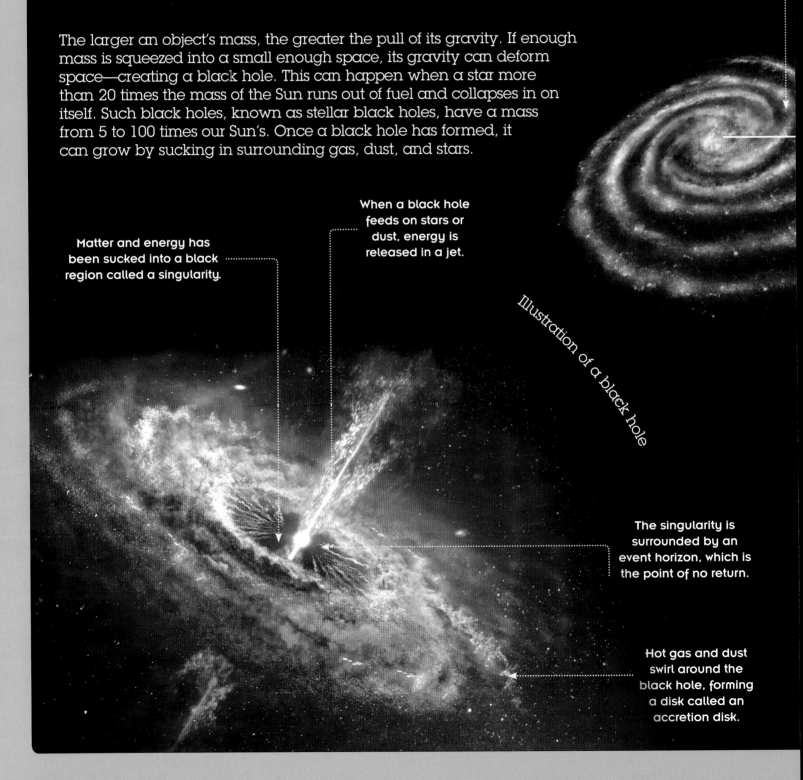

Matter and energy has been sucked into a black region called a singularity.

When a black hole feeds on stars or dust, energy is released in a jet.

Illustration of a black hole

The singularity is surrounded by an event horizon, which is the point of no return.

Hot gas and dust swirl around the black hole, forming a disk called an accretion disk.

At the core of our Milky Way Galaxy is a supermassive black hole with a mass 4 million times our Sun's.

Several stars closely orbit the black hole.

The supermassive black hole is called Sagittarius A*.

Sagittarius A* supermassive black hole

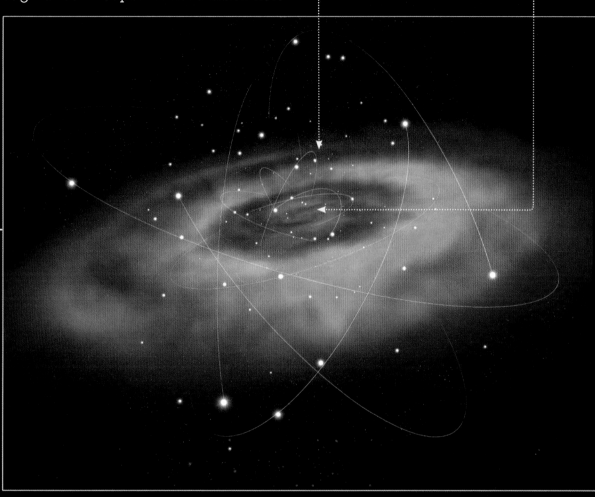

A supermassive black hole has a mass millions or billions of times the Sun's. A supermassive black hole is believed to lie at the core of most galaxies. Supermassive black holes may have formed from the growth of stellar black holes, from many black holes merging, from the collapse of whole star clusters, or from the collapse of gas clouds early in the life of the Universe.

First photo of a black hole

In 2017–19, the Event Horizon Telescope captured this image of the supermassive black hole at the core of galaxy M87.

We can see the black hole only because of the hot gas swirling around its event horizon.

Chapter 4

Universe of Galaxies

A galaxy is a collection of stars, planets, gas, and dust that is held together by gravity. Our own galaxy, the Milky Way, is one of up to 2 trillion galaxies in the Universe. Galaxies usually group together into clusters and, even larger, superclusters.

Everything with mass (or weight) has gravity, a force that pulls other objects toward it. The mass of the stars and other matter in a galaxy keeps it together. Everything in a galaxy spins around its central point, in the same way the planets in our Solar System spin around the Sun. At the heart of most galaxies, astronomers believe there is a supermassive black hole, a region with so much mass it has extremely powerful gravity.

Most galaxies are 3,000 to 300,000 light years across. A light year is the distance that light travels in a year: 9.46 trillion km (5.88 trillion miles). The stars around our Sun are mostly no closer than 4 light years apart, but in the core of a galaxy they can be 300 times closer. Most galaxies are separated from each other by at least 3,000,000 light years. The space between galaxies is not entirely empty: There are atoms of gas, perhaps one tiny atom in each 1 cubic m (35 cu ft) of space.

Astronomers are not sure how the first galaxies formed. It is possible that immense clumps of gas and dust collapsed, forming all the stars of a galaxy nearly at once. Another theory is that clusters of stars formed first, then grouped together.

As far as we can see from Earth, the Universe is currently 93 billion light years across.

The Universe

The Laniakea Supercluster

Earth

The Solar System

The Milky Way

The Local Group

Dark Matter

Matter is any substance, from an atom to a planet, that occupies space and has mass. However, around 85 percent of the matter in the Universe is invisible: it is called dark matter. We know dark matter exists because of the effects of its gravity. Astronomer Vera Rubin worked out there is a lot of dark matter in galaxies, because without its gravity, galaxies would fly apart.

Vera Rubin (1928–2016) found the first proof of dark matter.

Around 23 million light years from Earth, the spiral Whirlpool Galaxy has a smaller companion galaxy (at lower left) named NGC 5195.

GALAXY TYPES

Galaxies range from dwarfs with a few hundred million stars to giants with a hundred trillion stars. Most galaxies are dwarfs, which often orbit around a larger galaxy. Astronomers group galaxies into three main shapes: spiral, elliptical, and irregular.

Spiral galaxies are shaped like a windmill. Almost flat arms of bright young stars turn around a central bulge of older stars. Some spiral galaxies, called barred spirals, have a bar-shaped band of stars that stretches to either side of the core, then blends into the spiral arms.

Spiral

The Pinwheel Galaxy has around 1 trillion stars and is 170,000 light years across.

Barred spiral

The barred spiral galaxy known as NGC 1300 lies about 61 million light years from Earth.

Elliptical galaxies are roughly the shape of a ball that has been flattened a little. They usually contain old stars. Elliptical galaxies can be any size, but the largest galaxies in the Universe are all elliptical. They may have been formed when two or more galaxies collided and merged.

Elliptical

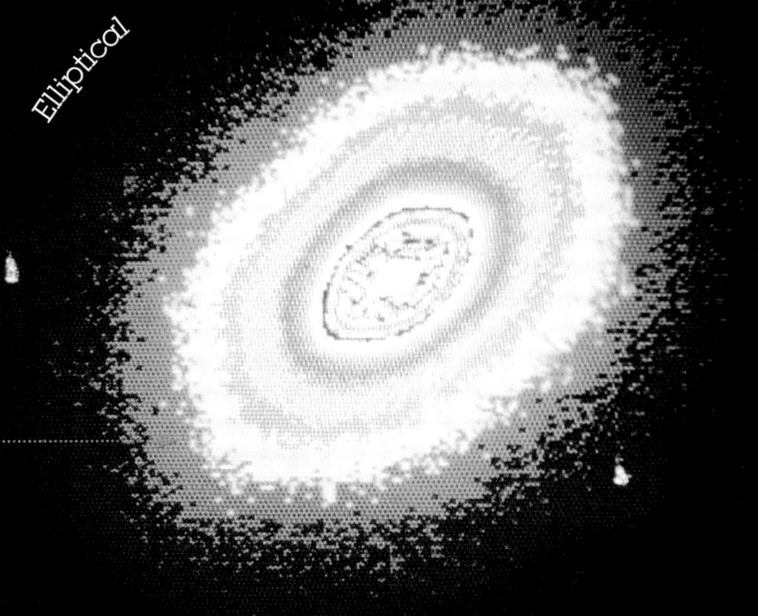

This photograph of galaxy M105 shows its brightest areas in yellow and its coolest in green.

Irregular

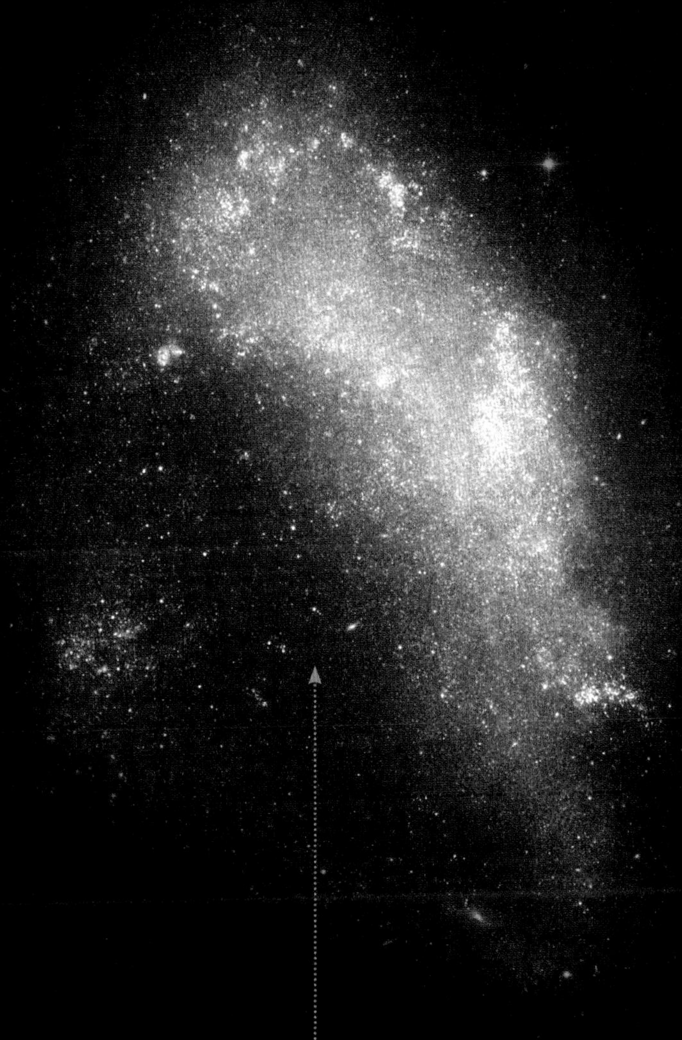

Around a quarter of galaxies do not have a regular elliptical or spiral shape. Irregular galaxies are usually dwarfs. They may have been pulled out of shape by the gravity of a larger galaxy nearby. Some galaxies, such as ring galaxies, have a peculiar shape because of a collision.

Hoag's Object is a ring galaxy that was formed 2 to 3 billion years ago when a small galaxy plunged through the heart of a larger disk-shaped galaxy.

Ring

NGC 1427A is a dwarf irregular galaxy that is pulled by the gravity of several nearby galaxies and will one day break apart.

THE MILKY WAY

Our Solar System is in a barred spiral galaxy known as the Milky Way. The stars, gas, and dust of the galaxy rotate around its core at different speeds, with the arms taking between 220 and 360 million years to make one orbit. Several smaller galaxies, called satellite galaxies, are in orbit around the Milky Way. The largest is the Large Magellanic Cloud, around 163,000 light years away.

The Perseus Arm, named after the constellation in which it can be seen from Earth, is one of two major arms.

The Milky Way

Globular clusters of stars orbit the galaxy.

The arms shine with the light of young blue stars, dotted with patches of hot red gas.

The Milky Way's disk is around 2,000 light years thick.

The Carina-Sagittarius Arm contains many hot young stars.

Our Solar System is in the minor Orion-Cygnus Arm, around 27,200 light years from the galaxy core.

The Milky Way

Type: Barred spiral galaxy

Size: 170,000–200,000 light years across

Number of Stars: 100–400 billion

Mass of Supermassive Black Hole: 10 million Suns

Satellite Galaxies: Up to 59

Average Rotation Speed: 210 km (130 miles) per second

Our galaxy can be seen as a pale milky band of light in the night sky, which is how it got its name.

The exact shape of the galaxy's arms is difficult to know because, from Earth, we cannot see across the tightly packed, dusty core to the other side.

The central bar is home to some of the oldest and yellowest stars, up to 13.5 billion years old, as well as a supermassive black hole called Sagittarius A*.

The major Scutum-Centaurus Arm spirals outward from the end of the central bar nearest to Earth.

In this photograph of the Andromeda Galaxy, one of its satellites, a dwarf elliptical galaxy called M110, can be seen as a bright oval to the lower left.

THE ANDROMEDA GALAXY

The Andromeda Galaxy is a barred spiral that formed 10 billion years ago when smaller galaxies collided. Today, Andromeda and our Milky Way are the two largest galaxies in a group known as the Local Group. There are at least 80 other galaxies in the group, all bound to each other by gravity.

On a moonless night, the Andromeda Galaxy is bright enough to be seen with the naked eye in the constellation of Andromeda. The constellation was named after a princess in Greek myths who was chained to a rock to be eaten by a sea monster. Andromeda was rescued by the hero Perseus, who appears in a nearby constellation.

In 964, Persian astronomer Abd al-Rahman al-Sufi was the first to record his findings about the Andromeda Galaxy, which he identified as a "cloud-like smear." Only in 1924 did the American astronomer Edwin Hubble prove that Andromeda was another galaxy, making it the first galaxy outside the Milky Way to be recognized.

The Local Group is around 9.8 million light years across. It contains two mini-groups of galaxies: the Milky Way and its satellites, and the Andromeda Galaxy and its satellites. The third largest galaxy in the group, Triangulum, may be a satellite of Andromeda's. It is the third and last spiral in the group, but it does not have a central bar.

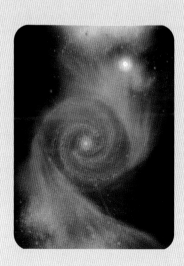

The constellation of Andromeda, its stars shown as gold dots, is pictured in Persian astronomer Abd al-Rahman al-Sufi's *Book of Fixed Stars*. The galaxy is just to the left of Princess Andromeda's belt.

The Andromeda Galaxy

Type: Barred spiral galaxy

Size: 220,000 light years across

Number of Stars: 1 trillion

Mass of Supermassive Black Hole: 110–230 million Suns

Satellite Galaxies: Up to 25

Average Distance from the Sun: 2.5 million light years

The Andromeda Galaxy is approaching the Milky Way at about 110 km (63 miles) per second, so in 4.5 billion years the two galaxies may collide.

EXOPLANETS

An exoplanet is a planet outside our Solar System. The first exoplanet was not discovered until 1992, but today we know of more than 4,000 exoplanets orbiting over 3,000 stars. All the exoplanets confirmed so far are in the Milky Way, due to the difficulty of spotting planets at the great distances of other galaxies.

Many different types of exoplanets have been found. There are small, rocky, Earth-like planets, as well as super-Earths, up to 10 times the mass of Earth. There are also ice giants, made of similar materials to our Solar System's Neptune and Uranus; and gas giants like Jupiter and Saturn. Hot Jupiters are gas giants which orbit so close to their star that they are very hot. Some exoplanets, known as rogue planets, do not orbit a star. They may have been thrown out of a solar system or they may have formed all alone.

Astronomers study exoplanets for signs they could be habitable, or suitable for life. To be habitable, a planet needs to be the right distance from its star for liquid water. If a planet is too close, water will boil away; if it is too distant, water will freeze. Liquid water is needed by all known life forms. This is because water is essential for transporting materials around the body. Several possibly habitable exoplanets have been found, but they are too far away to know if life has evolved there.

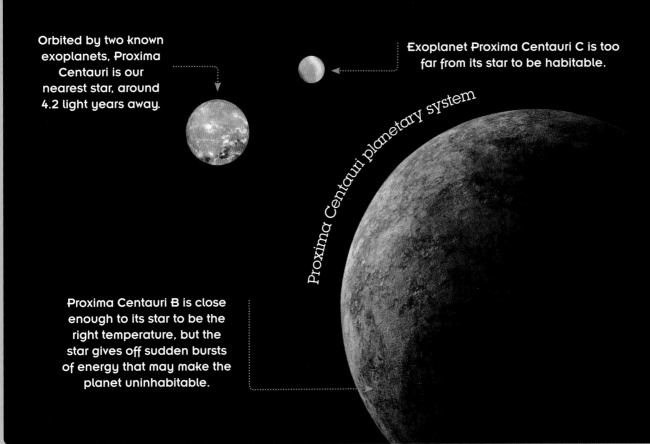

Orbited by two known exoplanets, Proxima Centauri is our nearest star, around 4.2 light years away.

Exoplanet Proxima Centauri C is too far from its star to be habitable.

Proxima Centauri planetary system

Proxima Centauri B is close enough to its star to be the right temperature, but the star gives off sudden bursts of energy that may make the planet uninhabitable.

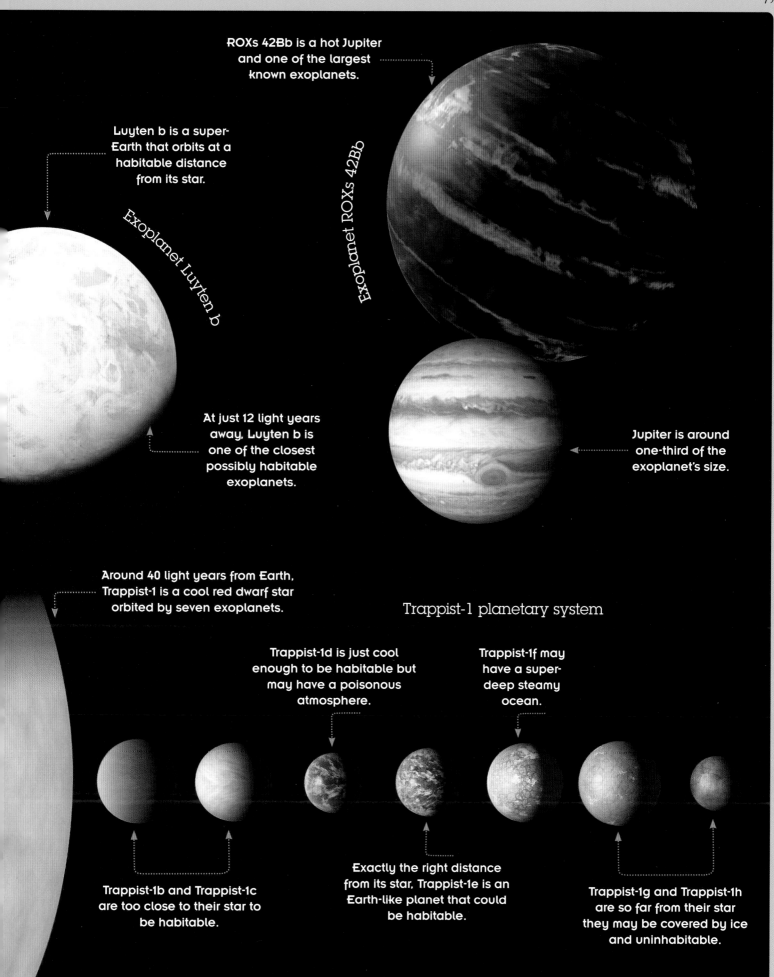

ROXs 42Bb is a hot Jupiter and one of the largest known exoplanets.

Luyten b is a super-Earth that orbits at a habitable distance from its star.

Exoplanet Luyten b

Exoplanet ROXs 42Bb

At just 12 light years away, Luyten b is one of the closest possibly habitable exoplanets.

Jupiter is around one-third of the exoplanet's size.

Around 40 light years from Earth, Trappist-1 is a cool red dwarf star orbited by seven exoplanets.

Trappist-1 planetary system

Trappist-1d is just cool enough to be habitable but may have a poisonous atmosphere.

Trappist-1f may have a super-deep steamy ocean.

Trappist-1b and Trappist-1c are too close to their star to be habitable.

Exactly the right distance from its star, Trappist-1e is an Earth-like planet that could be habitable.

Trappist-1g and Trappist-1h are so far from their star they may be covered by ice and uninhabitable.

THE ANTENNAE GALAXIES

The Antennae Galaxies are a pair of interacting galaxies. This means that the galaxies are being disturbed by each other's gravity. The galaxies get their name from the long trails of stars, gas, and dust thrown out by the interaction. These trails look a little like an insect's curving antennae, or feelers.

Interaction between galaxies may be minor, as when a satellite galaxy attracts the arm of the large galaxy it orbits. A more major interaction can result in galaxy "cannibalism," when a large galaxy drags away all the stars from a satellite. In the case of the Antennae Galaxies, the two galaxies are colliding. Most galaxies collide with another at some point, including our Milky Way, which will one day join with Andromeda.

Before the collision, the Antennae Galaxies, known as NGC 4038 and NGC 4039, were both spirals. Around 600 million years ago, the two galaxies passed through each other, leading to the "antennae" of stars thrown out by conflicting gravity pulls.

At the moment, the galaxies are going through a starburst phase, which is when many stars form at once: The collision of dust and gas clouds is causing clumps that grow,

get hotter, and become stars. In another 400 million years, the cores of the two galaxies will join. The galaxies will be merged as one giant, probably elliptical, galaxy.

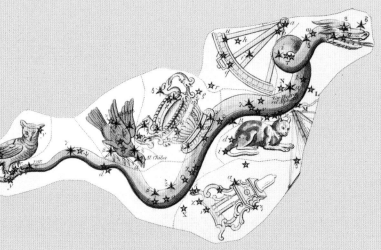

The Antennae Galaxies can be seen with a telescope in the constellation of Corvus, the crow, seen here in a 19th-century star chart.

The Antennae Galaxies

Type: Interacting galaxies

Size: 500,000 light years across

Number of Stars: 300 billion

Mass of Supermassive Black Holes: Not known

Satellite Galaxies: None known

Average Distance from the Sun: 45 million light years

The galaxies' long antennae can be seen through a powerful amateur telescope.

Star-forming regions of the Antennae Galaxies shine blue among patches of hot hydrogen gas, shown in pink.

This image, created by an X-ray telescope and a visible light telescope, shows Centaurus A's energy jets in blue.

CENTAURUS A

When dust, gas, and stars are sucked into the supermassive black hole at the heart of the Centaurus A galaxy, powerful jets of energy shoot out. Much of this energy is in the form of X-rays and radio waves, which makes Centaurus A a radio galaxy. Radio galaxies are one type of active galaxy.

Although most galaxies have a supermassive black hole at their core, the black hole in an active galaxy is particularly busy. It drags in material from the galaxy's central region. The material spins round and round the black hole, getting extremely hot. This throws out beams of energy.

A radio galaxy is a type of active galaxy that emits energy we detect as radio waves. A quasar is an active galaxy that emits light, radio waves, and other energy. Quasars are the brightest objects in the Universe, brighter than all the stars in the Milky Way, but they are nearly all too distant to be seen with amateur telescopes. A blazar is an active galaxy with a jet pointing straight at us.

At 11 million light years away, Centaurus A is the closest active galaxy to Earth. It is believed that, early in the Universe, most galaxies were active, but they have since quietened down. The reason why active galaxies are all so far away is that we are seeing these galaxies as they were when they were much younger. The more distant the object, the longer its light takes to reach us. We are seeing Centaurus A as it was 11 million years ago.

Jet

Black hole

Centaurus A emits jets of radio waves, X-rays, and infrared light.

Centaurus A

Type: Radio galaxy

Size: 60,000 light years across

Number of Stars: 300 billion

Mass of Supermassive Black Hole: 55 million Suns

Satellite Galaxies: Up to 28

Average Distance from the Sun: 11 million light years

This close-up shows the dark dust and glowing star clusters of a region of Centaurus A which is 8,500 light years wide.

STEPHAN'S QUINTET

Stephan's Quintet is a visual grouping of five galaxies. In a visual grouping, the objects appear close together in the night sky, although they may be hundreds of millions of light years apart. Yet four of the five galaxies in the quintet (meaning "group of five") are truly close to each other, forming a compact group of galaxies.

The quintet is named after the astronomer who first spotted it, Édouard Stephan, in 1877. While galaxy groups usually contain around 50 galaxies, a compact galaxy group has only around 5. These small groups reveal the importance of dark matter (see page 67) because, without it, they would not have enough mass—and enough gravity—to stay together.

One of the galaxies in the quintet, NGC 7320 (at upper left in the photograph on the right) is not part of the compact group, but lies 260 million light years away. It appears to be a member because it lies in our line of sight as we observe the group from Earth. The true members of the compact group are: NGC 7319 (at top right), a barred spiral that is being dragged out of shape by the gravity of the other galaxies; NGC 7318 A and B (in the middle), which look like one galaxy but are a pair of colliding galaxies; and NGC 7318

(at bottom left), an elliptical galaxy. The compact group will one day merge into an elliptical galaxy.

Stephan's Quintet is in the constellation of Pegasus, the winged horse, drawn here in a 17th-century Persian book.

Stephan's Quintet

Type: Compact group (and visual companion)

Size: 50 million light years across

Brightest Galaxy: NGC 7318 B

Largest Galaxy: NGC 7319

Average Distance from the Sun: 300 million light years

NGC 7318 B is being pulled into the middle of the group at millions of kilometers an hour, creating a shockwave that can be seen in this photograph as a blue curve of light.

The four members of the Stephan's Quintet compact group are much redder, because of their older stars, than the closer galaxy at top left, where young stars sparkle in blue.

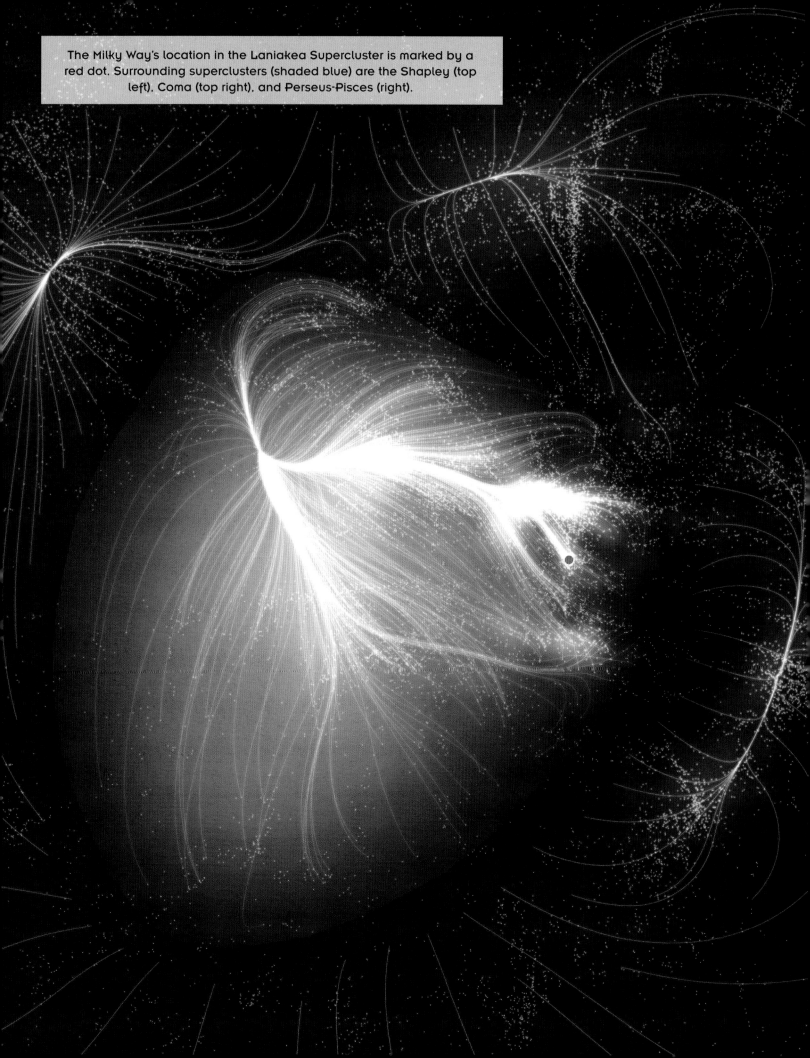

The Milky Way's location in the Laniakea Supercluster is marked by a red dot. Surrounding superclusters (shaded blue) are the Shapley (top left), Coma (top right), and Perseus-Pisces (right).

THE LANIAKEA SUPERCLUSTER

The Milky Way is a member of the Local Group of galaxies, which forms part of the Virgo Supercluster. This supercluster is just one portion of an even more immense cluster called the Laniakea Supercluster, containing 100,000 galaxies. Laniakea means "immense heaven" in Hawaiian.

At the Laniakea Supercluster's heart is a region called the Great Attractor, which has a huge gravitational pull. In the illustration opposite, the Laniakea is shaded in gold, while known galaxies are dots. The lines show the directions in which galaxies are being pulled toward the Great Attractor, where the brightest lines cross.

Despite the Great Attractor, the Laniakea is expanding. The Universe itself is expanding (see page 84) and, as it grows, so do superclusters. Like dots drawn on a balloon that is being blown up, the galaxy groups inside a supercluster get farther away from each other.

There may be around 10 million superclusters in the Universe. Superclusters are not evenly spread through the Universe. There are voids, or areas of nearly empty space, between them.

Superclusters collect together in incredibly long threads called filaments. This gives the Universe a structure a little like a sponge. This structure was caused by rippling differences in temperature as the Universe expanded after the Big Bang (see page 84).

This illustration shows how galaxies (red) are grouped into filaments in a cube of space billions of light years across.

Laniakea

Type: Supercluster

Size: 520 million light years across

Number of Galaxies: 100,000

Mass: 100 quadrillion (1 followed by 17 zeros) Suns

Distance of Great Attractor from the Sun:
250 million light years

The Great Attractor lies in this region of sky, in the Southern Triangle constellation.

FOCUS ON:

THE BIG BANG

Astronomers believe the Universe was born 13.8 billion years ago in an event called the Big Bang. In the first moment, the Universe began to expand from a single point—and has been expanding ever since. The Big Bang brought space and time into existence. No one knows why the Big Bang happened or what, if anything, existed beforehand.

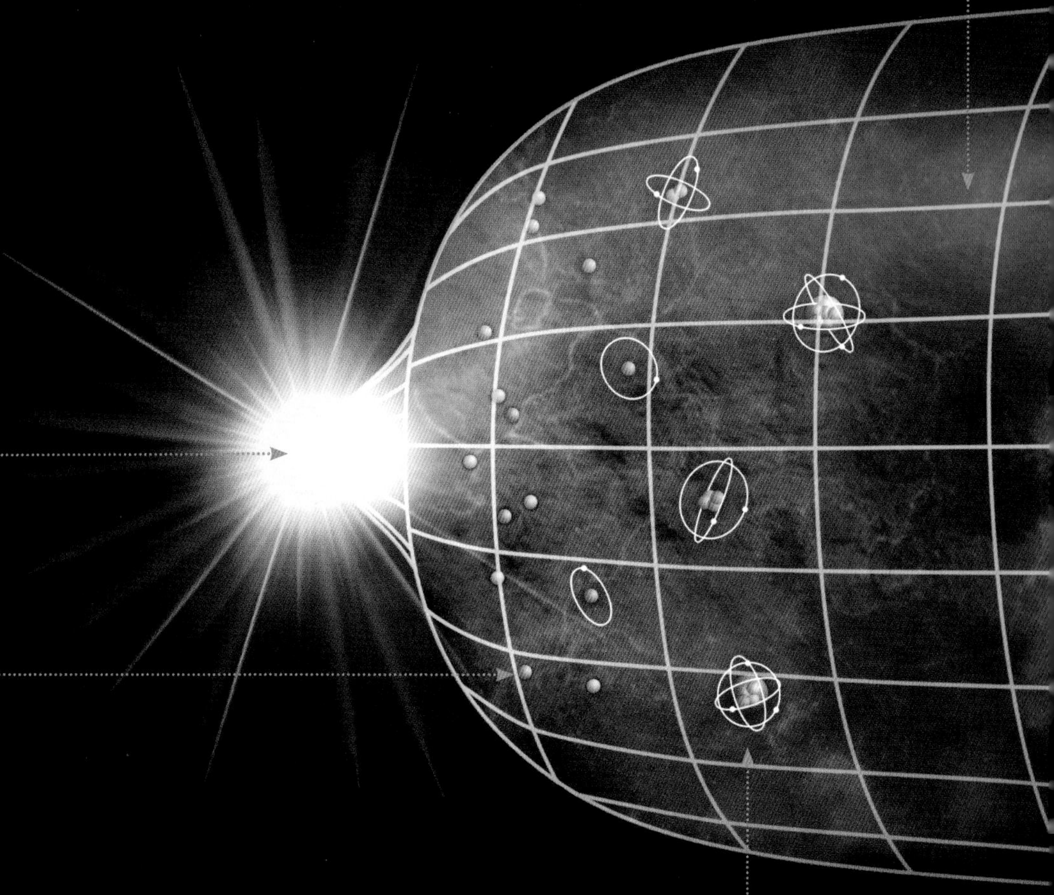

The Universe is born from a very hot, very dense (or tightly packed) point. In the next fraction of a second, the Universe doubles in size many times over, before settling down to a slower growth rate.

1 second: The Universe is a hot, soupy fog of tiny particles such as electrons, protons, and neutrons.

370,000 years: Electrons combine with protons and neutrons to form atoms, mostly of hydrogen and helium. Atoms are the building blocks for all matter.

Most astronomers think the Big Bang theory is correct because they can scan the sky to see the remains of the heat from the Big Bang as a form of energy called microwaves. They can also study how the Universe is growing and then use mathematics to "rewind" to the moment when it was a pinprick.

400 million years:
The first galaxies form.

10 million years: In the period known as the Dark Age, the Universe has cooled enough for light to travel, but there is not yet any source of light.

9.8 billion years:
The Universe starts to expand more quickly (giving this illustration its bell shape), due to the effects of dark energy, an unknown form of energy that pushes (or perhaps pulls) things away from each other.

Astronomers have many different theories about what will happen to the Universe in the future. Most believe it will continue to expand forever. However, some think the Universe will end in a Big Crunch, when it will shrink back to a point. A Big Bounce might follow, when the expansion starts all over again.

13.8 billion years:
The present day.

200 million years:
Gravity pulls clumps of hydrogen and helium gas into the first stars.

9.2 billion years:
Our Solar System forms. At first, Earth is a molten ball of rock.

In this timeline of the expansion of the Universe, the height of the bell-shaped area represents the size of the Universe. It is not drawn to scale.

Chapter 5

WATCHING THE SKY

Humans have always watched the night sky. At first, we believed the stars and planets were gods. We believed the Earth was still while the heavenly bodies moved around us. It took thousands of years to develop the mathematics and technology to begin to understand the Universe.

To someone looking at the night sky from Earth, the stars and planets appear to be fixed onto the inner surface of a ball. Astronomers call this ball the celestial sphere. Although the celestial sphere is imaginary, it is a useful idea for astronomers because they can "mark" it with a grid and then give coordinates for any object in the night sky.

When watching the night sky, it seems as if the stars rotate around us once a day. In fact, this seeming motion is caused by Earth's daily rotation round its own axis. Over the course of a year, the Sun seems to move along a path, called the ecliptic, in front of the background of stars. This seeming motion is actually caused by the Earth's yearly rotation round the Sun.

The planets also stay on the ecliptic, because they are all orbiting the Sun in the same plane (since they formed from the same flat disk of dust and gas). Unlike the Sun, the planets do not always move in the same direction along the ecliptic. Mercury and Venus are closer to the Sun than Earth, so they orbit it faster. As we watch, they make rings round the Sun, sometimes moving in the same direction and sometimes seeming to move the opposite way. The other planets orbit the Sun more slowly than Earth. When we move between one of these planets and the Sun, we see it appear to go backward because we are moving faster.

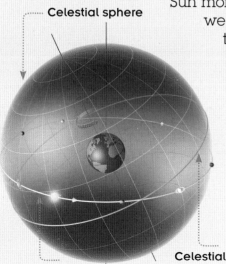

Celestial sphere

Ecliptic

Celestial equator

In this diagram of the celestial sphere, the ecliptic is drawn in yellow. The ecliptic is tilted away from the equator, or midline, of the celestial sphere because Earth's axis is slightly tilted.

Naming and Numbering

Astronomers have developed many systems for naming objects in the night sky. One of the most common is based on the *New General Catalogue of Nebulae and Clusters of Stars* (or NGC), compiled by John Louis Emil Dreyer in 1888. It gives an NGC number to 7,840 galaxies, star clusters, and nebulae. Another system is based on the Messier list of 110 objects, giving each an M number.

Thanks to Charles Messier (1730–1817), the Andromeda Galaxy can be called M31 by astronomers who speak many different languages.

Taken over several hours, this photograph shows the stars' apparent nightly movement. On the equator, the stars rise in the east and set in the west. Farther away from the equator (as pictured), stars rise and set at an angle to the horizon and some stay always hidden from view.

X-rays enter the telescope through the mirror assembly window, beneath its sunshade. The satellite is powered by solar panels.

THE CHANDRA X-RAY OBSERVATORY

Chandra is a telescope that records X-rays, a form of energy invisible to the human eye. Since most X-rays are absorbed by Earth's atmosphere, Chandra is on a satellite that orbits above it. The telescope is named after Indian-American astronomer Subrahmanyan Chandrasekhar.

Visible light is just one form of energy given off by stars, black holes, and other objects. The whole range of this energy is called the electromagnetic spectrum. Energy travels through space rather like waves across the ocean. When studying the waves, we can note their wavelength, which is the distance between the peak of one wave and the next.

Visible light is in the middle of the electromagnetic spectrum, with shorter wavelengths than radio waves but longer wavelengths than X-rays. Stars give off most of their energy as visible light. With their long wavelengths, radio waves, microwaves, and infrared have the lowest energy. They come from the coolest, darkest regions of space. At the other end of the spectrum are X-rays and gamma rays, which have very high energy. X-rays

come from super-hot spinning neutron stars and the material circling black holes.

Chandra uses mirrors to direct X-rays through gratings containing thousands of narrow openings, which divide the rays by wavelength. A detector then records the position of each X-ray and its energy level. Together, this builds up a picture of the object that is emitting X-rays.

X-rays

Ultraviolet

Visible light

Gamma rays

Infrared

Microwaves

Radio waves

In the middle of the electromagnetic spectrum is visible light, made up of all the shades of the rainbow. When sunlight is split by raindrops, our eyes and brain see the different wavelengths of visible light as different shades.

Chandra X-Ray Observatory

Type: X-ray space telescope

Size of Main Mirror: 1.2 m (3.9 ft) across

Focal Length: 10 m (32.8 ft)

Average Distance from Earth: 80,000 km (50,000 miles)

Launch: 1999

Built by: National Aeronautics and Space Administration (NASA) and other US organizations

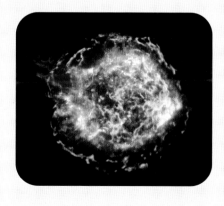

Chandra created this image of the X-rays coming from an exploded star, the supernova remnant Cassiopeia A.

ASTRONOMERS

In ancient civilizations from Babylon to India, China, and Central America, the earliest astronomers were often priests. As they studied movements in the night sky, they also searched for signs from the gods. Today, astronomers are scientists who observe, calculate, and test—but they still find mysteries to be solved.

More than 3,000 years ago, Babylonian astronomers watched the movements of the Sun and Moon, then used mathematics to create calendars to help with the farming year. In ancient Greece, from the 4th century BCE, astronomers started to use geometry, the mathematics of shapes, to work out the circumference of the Earth and distances to the Sun and Moon.

The Babylonian sun-god Shamash holds a coiled rope and a measuring rod.

Babylonian calendar

The Persian astronomer Al-Sufi (903–986) published a book containing maps of 48 star constellations.

The writing gives the time of rising of three stars in each month.

Abd al-Rahman al-Sufi

Copernicus (1473–1543) developed the theory that Earth moves round the Sun. It took over a century for the theory to be widely accepted.

The first woman to receive a salary as a scientist, German astronomer Caroline Herschel (1750–1848) discovered several comets.

Nicolaus Copernicus

Caroline Herschel

Most ancient Greek astronomers believed the Earth was stationery at the heart of the Universe, with all other objects moving around it. One of the first to suggest this idea was wrong was Nicolaus Copernicus, who used his studies of the movements of planets to prove that the Sun was at the middle of the Solar System. This was the start of a new era in astronomy, where the scientific method led the way: Careful observation suggests new ideas, or theories, which are tested by more observation. Through the scientific method, we know about black holes, which were predicted by Albert Einstein through mathematics in 1915, but not actually observed in a photograph until 2019.

Albert Einstein

Nancy Roman

Albert Einstein (1879–1955) used mathematics to reveal the relationships between space, time, and the structure of the Universe.

As Chief of Astronomy at NASA, Nancy Roman (1925–2018) planned the Hubble Space Telescope, which helped us calculate the age of the Universe.

The James Webb Space Telescope

This telescope will observe the Universe in visible light and infrared. It is intended to take over from the Hubble Space Telescope, which was launched in 1990, but will be able to see even more distant objects. It is named after the NASA administrator who oversaw the United States' earliest space flights.

When objects are very distant, their light is stretched to a longer wavelength (see page 91) as it travels toward us. This means that energy which was originally visible light looks like infrared or radio waves by the time it reaches us. By observing infrared, the Webb Telescope will be able to see some of the most distant objects in the Universe. Since they are so distant, their light will have taken billions of years to reach the telescope. As a result, the telescope will capture images that show what was happening in the very earliest days of the Universe, such as the formation of the first galaxies.

To observe infrared, which can be felt as heat, the Webb Telescope needs to be kept very cold. If not, its own instruments would send out infrared waves that would overwhelm it. The telescope has its own sunshade to keep the instruments below -223°C (-370°F). In addition, the Webb Telescope will be in orbit round the Sun rather than the Earth, but will stay in Earth's shadow at all times.

Primary mirror

Secondary mirror

Sunshade

The main mirror is made of 18 gold-plated hexagonal segments.

James Webb Space Telescope

Type: Infrared and optical space telescope

Size of Main Mirror: 6.5 m (21 ft) across

Focal Length: 131 m (431 ft)

Average Distance from Earth:
  1.5 million km (930,000 miles)

Launch: 2021

Built by: NASA, European Space Agency (ESA), and Canadian Space Agency (CSA)

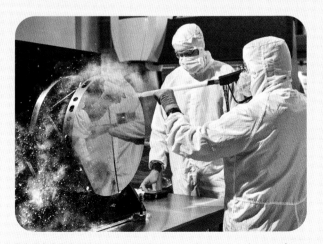

Engineers clean the telescope's secondary mirror.

Scientists examine the segments of the James Webb Telescope's main mirror before launch.

CONSTELLATIONS

A constellation is a group of stars that appear to form the pattern of a person, animal, or object. Today's astronomers agree on 88 official constellations, including 48 that were named by the ancient Greeks after figures from their myths. Well-known patterns within constellations, such as the "Big Dipper," are called asterisms.

The constellations are a useful way for astronomers to describe the location of an object, such as a galaxy, that appears to lie in a particular constellation. There are several methods for identifying the stars in a constellation, including the Bayer system, which gives each star a letter of the Greek alphabet, starting with the brightest in the constellation: alpha.

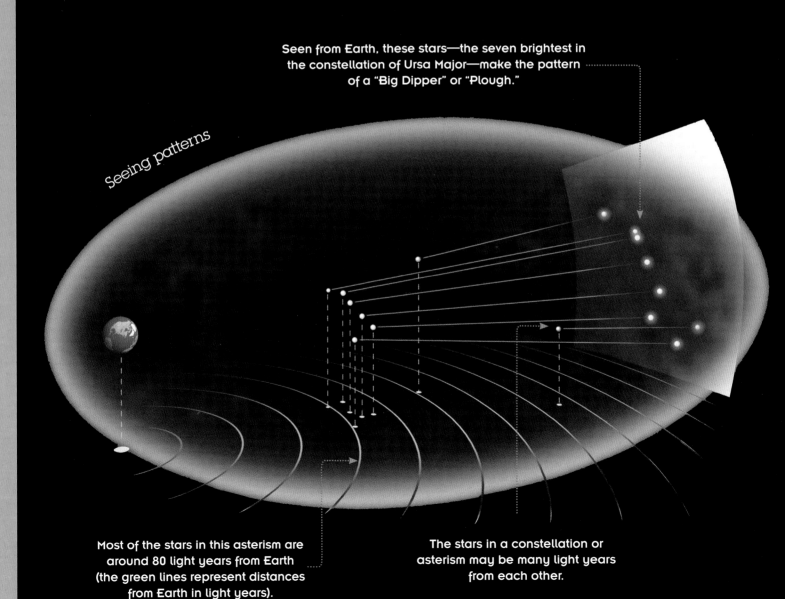

Seen from Earth, these stars—the seven brightest in the constellation of Ursa Major—make the pattern of a "Big Dipper" or "Plough."

Seeing patterns

Most of the stars in this asterism are around 80 light years from Earth (the green lines represent distances from Earth in light years).

The stars in a constellation or asterism may be many light years from each other.

Through the year, the Sun seems to pass through 12 constellations along the ecliptic, its path round the celestial sphere (see page 86). These are known as the constellations of the zodiac (from the ancient Greek for "little animals").

The zodiac constellations

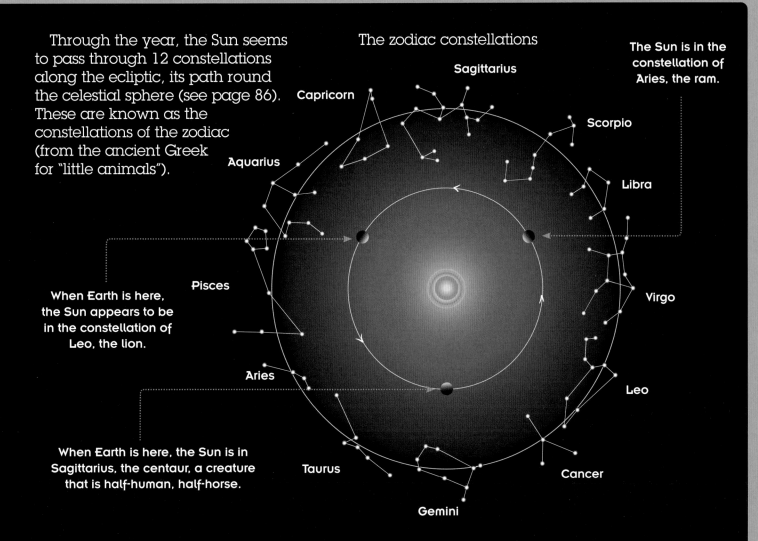

The Sun is in the constellation of Aries, the ram.

When Earth is here, the Sun appears to be in the constellation of Leo, the lion.

When Earth is here, the Sun is in Sagittarius, the centaur, a creature that is half-human, half-horse.

Sagittarius

Capricorn

Aquarius

Pisces

Aries

Taurus

Gemini

Cancer

Leo

Virgo

Libra

Scorpio

The North Star, also known as Polaris, lies on the North Pole of the celestial sphere, making it a useful way to find the direction of north at night. The North Star is the brightest star in the constellation of Ursa Minor, the little bear. The South Star, also known as Polaris Australis, is in the constellation of Octans, but its faintness makes it difficult to spot.

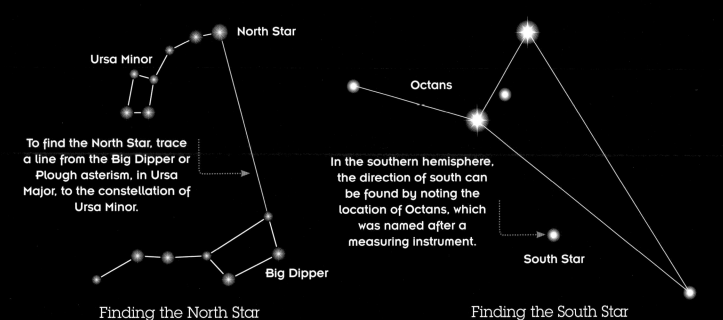

North Star

Ursa Minor

To find the North Star, trace a line from the Big Dipper or Plough asterism, in Ursa Major, to the constellation of Ursa Minor.

Big Dipper

Octans

In the southern hemisphere, the direction of south can be found by noting the location of Octans, which was named after a measuring instrument.

South Star

Finding the North Star

Finding the South Star

In 2017, just a year after starting work, Eye in the Sky discovered two new pulsars, named FAST pulsars #1 and #2.

EYE OF THE SKY

Eye of the Sky, officially known as FAST (Five-hundred-meter Aperture Spherical radio Telescope), is in the hills of Guizhou, China. Its 500-m (1,600-ft) wide bowl-shaped dish, the largest of its type, gathers radio waves from objects such as pulsars, which are the spinning cores of collapsed supergiant stars.

The dish of a radio telescope acts like the mirror in a reflecting telescope. It reflects and focuses radio waves onto a device called a receiving antenna. FAST's receiver hangs 140 m (459 ft) above the dish, giving a focal length of 140 m (459 ft). The receiver amplifies (or increases) the radio waves, which are recorded so they can be studied on a computer.

Since the radio waves from distant objects are very weak, large dishes are needed to collect enough radio energy to study them. Radio telescopes are located away from cities and towns, so that radios and other machines cannot disturb them.

The FAST dish is fixed in a natural valley so, unlike smaller, steerable radio telescopes, it cannot turn to face any point in the sky.

However, the dish is made of 4,450 triangular metal panels that can be tilted to face particular objects, as long as they are not too close to the horizon.

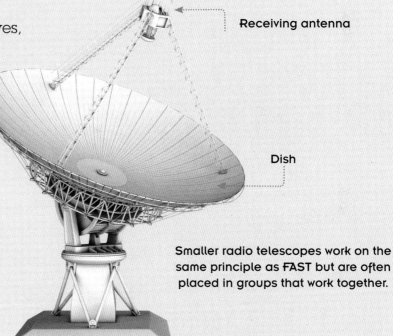

Receiving antenna

Dish

Smaller radio telescopes work on the same principle as FAST but are often placed in groups that work together.

Eye of the Sky (FAST)

Type: Radio telescope

Size of Dish: 500 m (1,600 ft) across

Focal Length: 140 m (459 ft)

Completed: 2016

Built by: Chinese National Astronomical Observatories (NAOC) and Chinese Academy of Sciences

This image shows the radio waves (in red) given off by galaxy NGC 5532.

COMETS

Comets are small, icy objects that travel inside our Solar System, with very elliptical (or stretched) orbits that take them both close to and far from the Sun. When comets near the Sun, they get hot and release gases. In most years, one comet can be seen with the naked eye, while several more can be watched with a store-bought telescope.

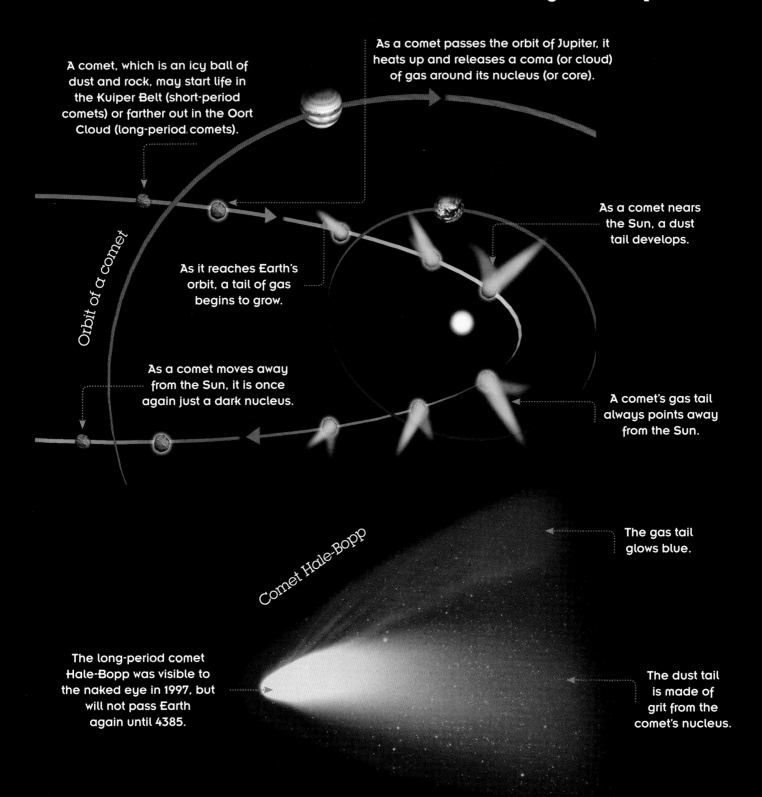

A comet, which is an icy ball of dust and rock, may start life in the Kuiper Belt (short-period comets) or farther out in the Oort Cloud (long-period comets).

As a comet passes the orbit of Jupiter, it heats up and releases a coma (or cloud) of gas around its nucleus (or core).

As a comet nears the Sun, a dust tail develops.

Orbit of a comet

As it reaches Earth's orbit, a tail of gas begins to grow.

As a comet moves away from the Sun, it is once again just a dark nucleus.

A comet's gas tail always points away from the Sun.

Comet Hale-Bopp

The gas tail glows blue.

The long-period comet Hale-Bopp was visible to the naked eye in 1997, but will not pass Earth again until 4385.

The dust tail is made of grit from the comet's nucleus.

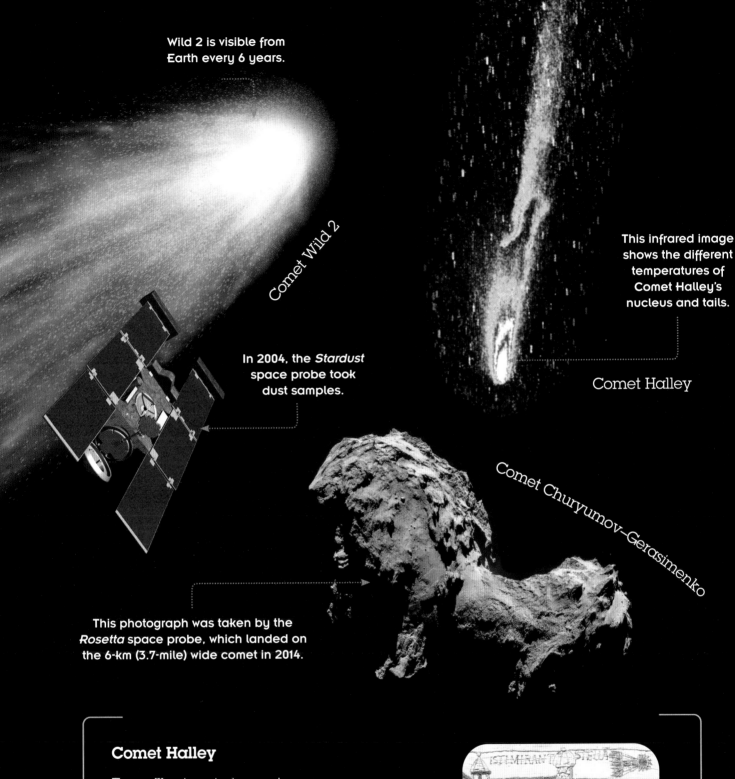

Wild 2 is visible from Earth every 6 years.

Comet Wild 2

This infrared image shows the different temperatures of Comet Halley's nucleus and tails.

Comet Halley

In 2004, the *Stardust* space probe took dust samples.

Comet Churyumov–Gerasimenko

This photograph was taken by the *Rosetta* space probe, which landed on the 6-km (3.7-mile) wide comet in 2014.

Comet Halley

Type: Short-period comet

Size of Nucleus: 11 km (6.8 miles) across

Speed when Closest to the Sun: 196,000 km (122,000 miles) per hour

Speed when Farthest from the Sun: 3,300 km (2,000 miles) per hour

Length of Orbit: 75 years

Next Seen from Earth: 2061

Comet Halley was seen from England in 1066, as shown in the Bayeux Tapestry (at top right).

THE PERSEIDS

A meteor shower is when a number of small rocky or metal objects, called meteoroids, enter Earth's atmosphere together. The meteoroids produce streaks of light known as meteors or shooting stars. The most spectacular meteor showers are the Perseids, which appear from the region of the Perseus constellation.

Most meteoroids are fragments of comets or asteroids. The Perseid meteoroids are dust thrown off by the Comet Swift–Tuttle. The shower can be seen every year in July and August, most easily from the northern hemisphere, as Earth's orbit brings it close to the comet's tail.

When a meteoroid enters Earth's atmosphere, friction with the air makes it heat up, a little like rubbing your hands together warms them up. This heat creates a streak of light and completely burns up smaller meteoroids. If any of a meteoroid survives long enough to hit the ground, it is called a meteorite. Comet dust, which causes most meteor showers, rarely survives its fall through the air. Most meteorites are the remains of asteroids.

Other well-known meteor showers are the Leonids in November, Geminids in December, Quadrantids in January, and Eta Aquariids in April–May. The Eta Aquariids, which come from the region of the Aquarius constellation, are caused by Comet Halley.

The Perseus constellation, named after a hero from Greek myths, is shown in a Persian manuscript with its stars in gold.

The Perseids

Type: Meteor shower

Comet of Origin: Swift–Tuttle

Constellation: Perseus

Speed of Meteors: 212,000 km (132,000 miles) per hour

Number of Meteors at Peak: 100 per hour

Dates: Mid-July–late August (peak around August 12)

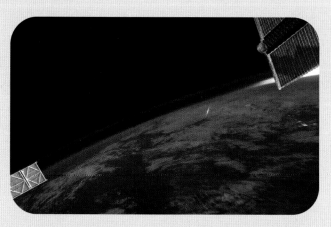

The Perseids were photographed by astronaut Ron Garan on board the International Space Station.

The Perseids are best viewed in the hours before dawn, far from the lights of cities and roads.

STAR CHARTS

These star charts show the constellations of the northern and southern celestial hemispheres (see page 86). Earth's movement around the Sun means that not every constellation in a hemisphere can be viewed all year from every location. Earth's rotation means that, once a day, the stars rotate around the north and south celestial poles.

The northern constellations are found in the northern hemisphere of the celestial sphere above the celestial equator. Most of the 36 modern northern constellations are based on those described by the ancient Greeks, which may have their roots thousands of years earlier, in Babylonian astronomy.

The Milky Way Galaxy snakes across the northern and southern skies as a paler band.

Ursa Major is the largest constellation in the northern hemisphere.

Coma Berenices, meaning "Berenice's hair," is named after Queen Berenice of Egypt, who gave her long hair as a gift to the gods.

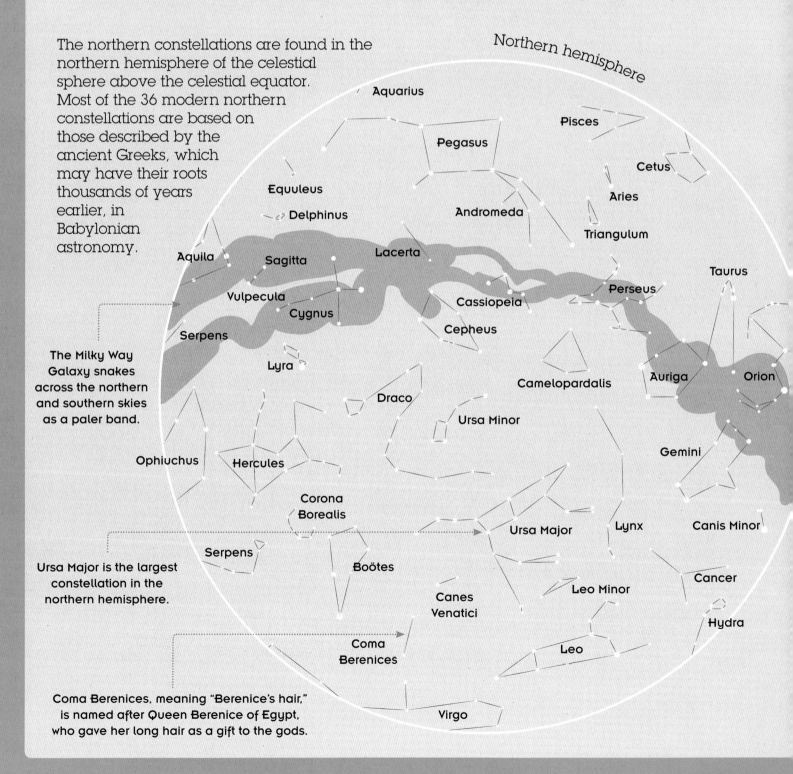

Northern hemisphere

Aquarius
Pisces
Pegasus
Cetus
Equuleus
Aries
Delphinus
Andromeda
Triangulum
Aquila
Lacerta
Taurus
Sagitta
Perseus
Vulpecula
Cassiopeia
Cygnus
Cepheus
Serpens
Camelopardalis
Lyra
Auriga
Orion
Draco
Ursa Minor
Gemini
Ophiuchus
Hercules
Corona Borealis
Ursa Major
Lynx
Canis Minor
Serpens
Boötes
Cancer
Leo Minor
Canes Venatici
Hydra
Coma Berenices
Leo
Virgo

There are 52 southern constellations. Most of the southern constellations are in regions of the sky not viewable from Europe, so they were not mapped by the ancient Greeks. Many were mapped from the 16th century, when European sailors journeyed south of the equator, although peoples of the southern hemisphere had long had their own names and stories about the stars.

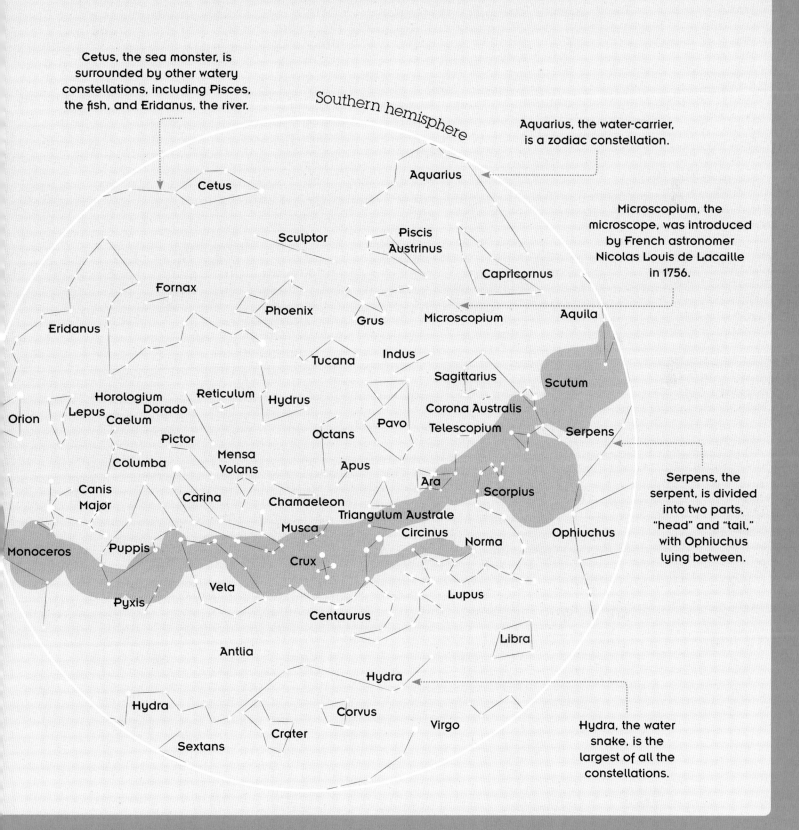

Cetus, the sea monster, is surrounded by other watery constellations, including Pisces, the fish, and Eridanus, the river.

Southern hemisphere

Aquarius, the water-carrier, is a zodiac constellation.

Microscopium, the microscope, was introduced by French astronomer Nicolas Louis de Lacaille in 1756.

Serpens, the serpent, is divided into two parts, "head" and "tail," with Ophiuchus lying between.

Hydra, the water snake, is the largest of all the constellations.

Cetus · Aquarius · Sculptor · Piscis Austrinus · Capricornus · Fornax · Phoenix · Grus · Microscopium · Aquila · Eridanus · Tucana · Indus · Sagittarius · Scutum · Horologium · Reticulum · Hydrus · Corona Australis · Orion · Lepus · Dorado · Pavo · Telescopium · Serpens · Caelum · Octans · Pictor · Mensa · Apus · Ara · Scorpius · Columba · Volans · Canis Major · Carina · Chamaeleon · Triangulum Australe · Ophiuchus · Monoceros · Musca · Circinus · Norma · Puppis · Crux · Vela · Lupus · Pyxis · Centaurus · Libra · Antlia · Hydra · Hydra · Corvus · Virgo · Crater · Sextans

Chapter 6

EXPLORING SPACE

The first human-made object in space was the Soviet Union's uncrewed *Sputnik 1* satellite, which orbited Earth in 1957. Since then, humans have walked on the Moon and sent uncrewed space probes to planets, moons, and comets in the distant Solar System.

The dividing line between Earth's atmosphere and outer space is said to be 100 km (62 miles) above Earth's surface. To explore space, humans had to build vehicles that could overcome the pull of Earth's gravity, the force that pulls us to the ground when we jump. By the middle of the 20th century, engineers had designed rockets that were powerful enough to lift spacecraft into space. Rockets push out super-hot gas behind them, which sends them upward at high speed. When a rocket has lifted its spacecraft high enough, the rocket falls back, often into the ocean.

For a spacecraft to escape Earth's gravity and fly into space, it must reach a speed of 40,320 km (25,039 miles) per hour. This is called the escape velocity. Satellites (objects in orbit) do not need to travel so fast, since a satellite needs to balance Earth's gravity rather than escape it. To orbit at 200 km (125 miles) above Earth's surface, the speed needed is 27,400 km (17,025 miles) per hour. Once a satellite has been taken to this speed by its rocket, the satellite can continue in a curved path, circling Earth, firing its own engines only to correct its course.

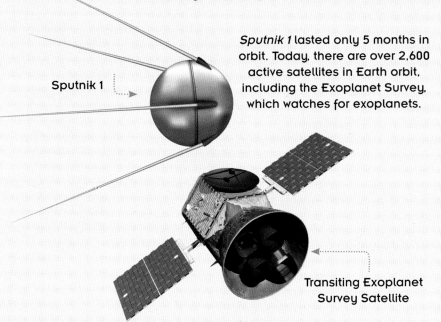

Sputnik 1

Sputnik 1 lasted only 5 months in orbit. Today, there are over 2,600 active satellites in Earth orbit, including the Exoplanet Survey, which watches for exoplanets.

Transiting Exoplanet
Survey Satellite

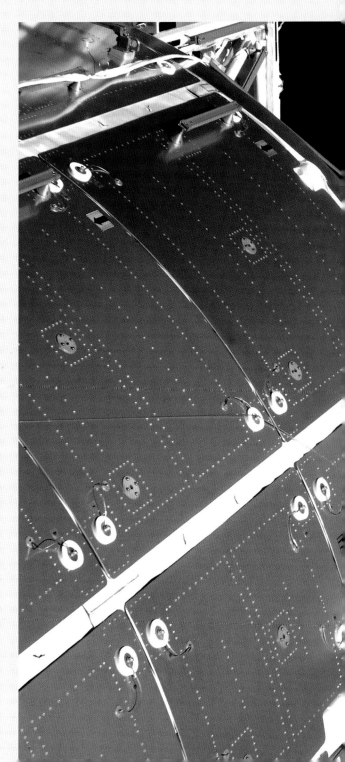

Astrodynamics

Astrodynamics is the study of how rockets and spacecraft move through space as they fire their engines and are pulled by the gravity of stars and planets. Astrodynamics is based on mathematical equations about motion, including the fact that a moving object will keep moving unless another force acts on it. Mathematician Katherine Johnson did the astrodynamics calculations that made possible the United States' first crewed space flights.

Katherine Johnson (1918–2020) worked out flight paths for the National Aeronautics and Space Administration (NASA).

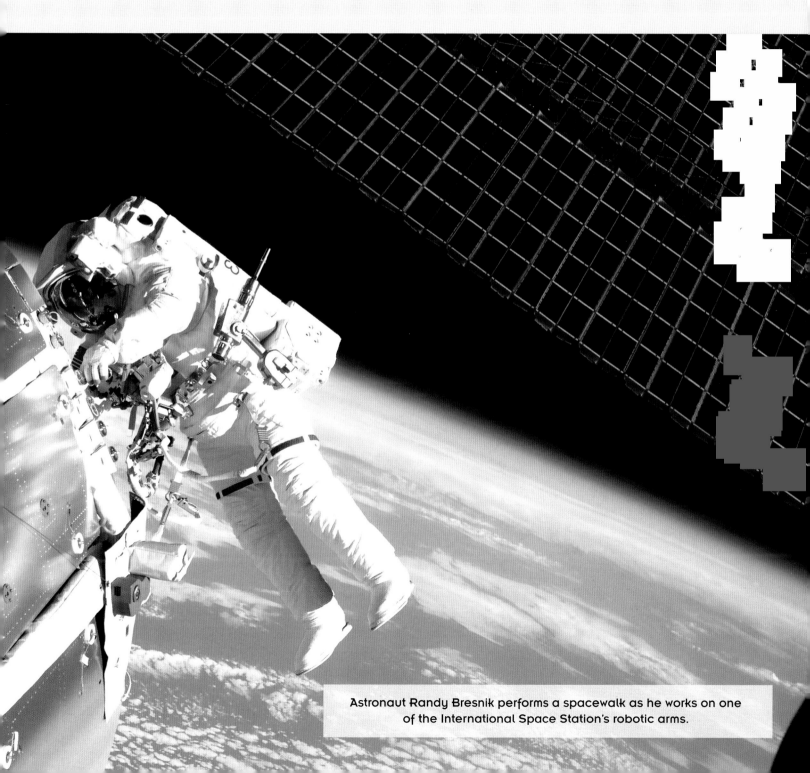

Astronaut Randy Bresnik performs a spacewalk as he works on one of the International Space Station's robotic arms.

This photograph of Buzz Aldrin on the Moon was taken by Neil Armstrong, whose reflection can be seen in Aldrin's visor.

APOLLO 11

On July 20, 1969, the Apollo 11 mission landed US astronauts Neil Armstrong and Edwin "Buzz" Aldrin on the Moon, while Michael Collins waited for them on board their command and service module in Moon orbit. Armstrong and Aldrin were the first and second humans to set foot on the Moon.

The United States' Apollo missions began in 1967 with the aim of putting the first humans on the Moon. It was only in 1961 that the Soviet Union had sent the first human into space, Yuri Gagarin (see page 122). Apollo 10, the mission before Apollo 11, had been a practice run for the Moon landing, successfully orbiting the Moon in May 1969.

The Apollo spacecraft had three parts: the command module, containing the astronauts' cabin; the service module, holding the engine; and the lunar module, for landing on the Moon. The mission began on July 16 when the spacecraft, carrying the three astronauts, was blasted into Earth orbit by a Saturn V rocket.

Around 2 hours after leaving Earth, the rocket had done its work, leaving Apollo to fly into Moon orbit alone. On July 20, Armstrong and Aldrin undocked the lunar module from the command and service module, then flew down to the Moon's surface. They spent 21 hours and 36 minutes on the Moon, taking photographs, doing experiments, and choosing rock samples.

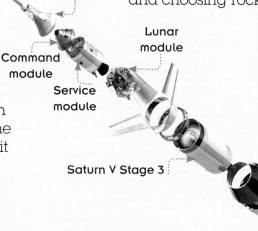

Launch escape system

Lunar module

Command module

Service module

Saturn V Stage 3

Saturn V Stage 2

Saturn V Stage 1

The Saturn V rocket had three stages. Each stage in turn fired its engines until it had used up its fuel and then separated, either falling into the ocean or staying in space.

Apollo 11

Type: Crewed Moon landing mission

Spacecraft: Apollo command and service module *Columbia* and Apollo lunar module *Eagle*

Rocket: Saturn V

Launch Date: July 16, 1969

Landing Site: Sea of Tranquillity

End of Mission: July 24, 1969

Operator: NASA

On July 24, having left the lunar module to crash into the Moon and the service module to burn up, the command module splashed down in the Pacific Ocean.

CREWED SPACECRAFT

Crewed spacecraft have never journeyed farther than the Moon. Most crewed spacecraft, apart from spaceplanes (see page 118), are space capsules. These are launched into Earth orbit by a rocket. After completing their mission, the crew descends in a wingless re-entry capsule, which lands in the ocean or desert, its fall slowed by parachutes and sometimes also engines.

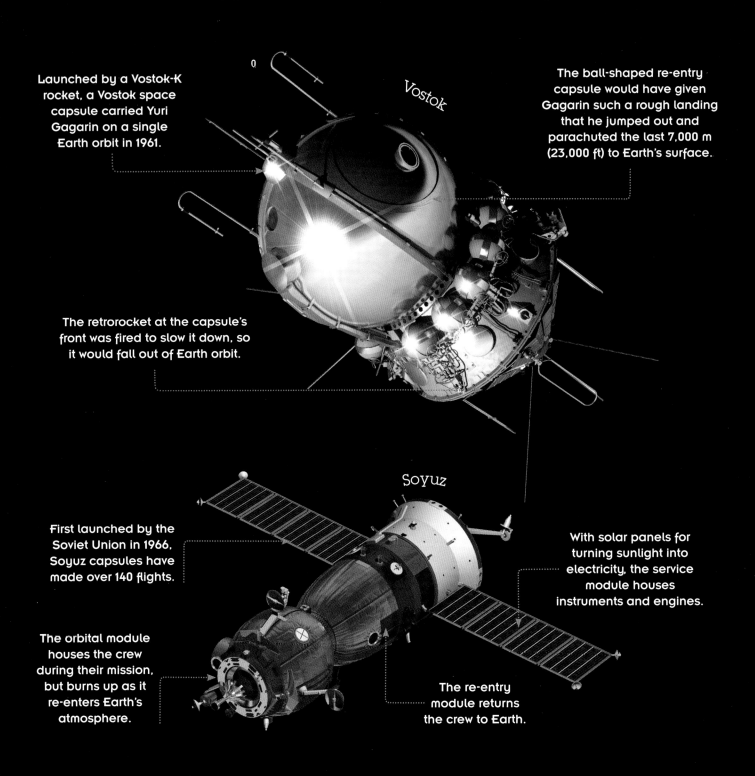

Vostok

Launched by a Vostok-K rocket, a Vostok space capsule carried Yuri Gagarin on a single Earth orbit in 1961.

The ball-shaped re-entry capsule would have given Gagarin such a rough landing that he jumped out and parachuted the last 7,000 m (23,000 ft) to Earth's surface.

The retrorocket at the capsule's front was fired to slow it down, so it would fall out of Earth orbit.

Soyuz

First launched by the Soviet Union in 1966, Soyuz capsules have made over 140 flights.

With solar panels for turning sunlight into electricity, the service module houses instruments and engines.

The orbital module houses the crew during their mission, but burns up as it re-enters Earth's atmosphere.

The re-entry module returns the crew to Earth.

Crew Dragon

Type: Partly reusable space capsule

Seats: 7

Size: 8 × 4 m (27 × 13 ft)

Engines: 16 Draco thrusters

Rocket: Falcon 9 Block 5

Launch Date: May 30, 2020

Operator: SpaceX Corp

Crew Dragon launches on top of a Falcon 9 rocket from NASA's Kennedy Space Center in Florida, USA.

The launch escape system carried three rockets that could be fired in an emergency to push the capsule away from its rocket.

This illustration shows the interior of the adapter module, which carried four spherical retrorockets.

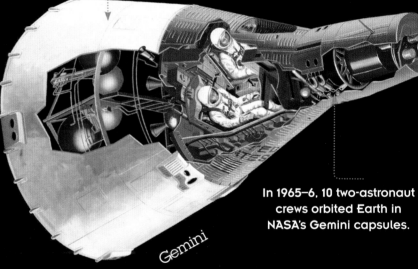

In 1965–6, 10 two-astronaut crews orbited Earth in NASA's Gemini capsules.

Gemini

The single-person Mercury crew compartment carried the first American into space, Alan Shepard, in 1961.

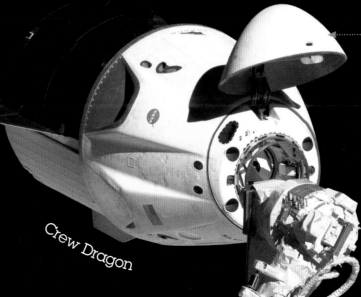

Crew Dragon's nose cone is open, revealing its docking mechanism, as it approaches the International Space Station.

Mercury

Crew Dragon

VENERA 9

In 1961, the Soviet Union launched its Venera program, with the aim of sending the first uncrewed spacecraft, known as a space probe, to another planet. They set their sights on Venus. In 1975, *Venera 9* returned the first photographs from the surface of another planet.

The Venera program achieved many "firsts" in space exploration. In 1961, *Venera 1* managed the first flyby of another planet. In 1966, *Venera 3* was the first probe to crash land on another planet. As planned, the mission's flyby probe detached the entry probe, which fell to the planet's surface. In 1970, *Venera 7* was the first probe to make a soft landing on another planet. Due to the temperature of 475°C (887°F) and the thickness of Venus's atmosphere, which put immense pressure on the probe, it survived for only 20 minutes.

The *Venera 9* mission was made up of a lander, built to withstand high pressure and heat, and an orbiter with powerful engines. While the lander dropped through Venus's atmosphere, the orbiter moved into orbit around the planet, examining Venus's clouds with its instruments.

The lander's fall was slowed by parachutes. It was also designed so that a hollow ring around its lower part was crushed as it hit the ground, absorbing most of the impact. For 53 minutes, *Venera 9* sent photographs of the surface by radio waves to the orbiter, which sent them on to Earth.

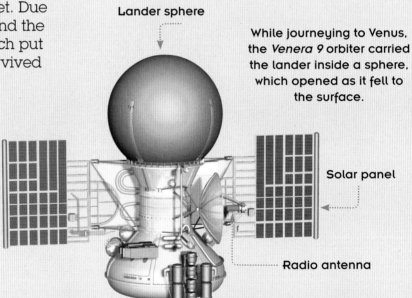

Lander sphere

While journeying to Venus, the *Venera 9* orbiter carried the lander inside a sphere, which opened as it fell to the surface.

Solar panel

Radio antenna

Venera 9

Type: Uncrewed Venus orbiter and lander mission

Spacecraft: 4MV planetary probe

Rocket: Proton-K

Launch Date: June 8, 1975

Landing Site: Near Beta Regio

End of Mission: March 22, 1976 (contact lost)

Operator: Soviet Union

This photograph taken by *Venera 9* shows flat rocks on Venus's surface.

This illustration imagines *Venera 9* on the Venusian surface shortly after landing. The probe is probably still on Venus today, although greatly damaged by heat and the acidity of the atmosphere.

SPACE PROBES

Space probes are uncrewed robotic spacecraft that travel where humans cannot currently go, because the journey or destination is too dangerous or too distant. Space probes can flyby, orbit, or land on planets, moons, comets, and asteroids, or even journey beyond the Solar System.

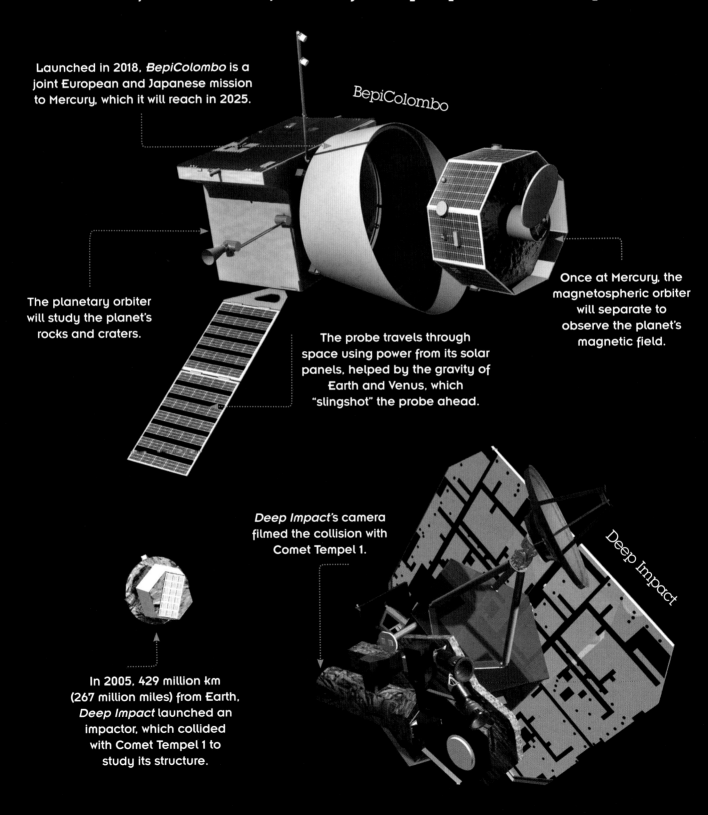

Launched in 2018, *BepiColombo* is a joint European and Japanese mission to Mercury, which it will reach in 2025.

BepiColombo

The planetary orbiter will study the planet's rocks and craters.

The probe travels through space using power from its solar panels, helped by the gravity of Earth and Venus, which "slingshot" the probe ahead.

Once at Mercury, the magnetospheric orbiter will separate to observe the planet's magnetic field.

Deep Impact's camera filmed the collision with Comet Tempel 1.

Deep Impact

In 2005, 429 million km (267 million miles) from Earth, *Deep Impact* launched an impactor, which collided with Comet Tempel 1 to study its structure.

Voyager 1

Type: Mariner Jupiter-Saturn space probe

Equipment: Cameras, plus instruments for studying magnetic fields, plasma, and cosmic rays

Size: 0.47 m × 1.78 m (1.5 ft × 5.8 ft) main body (not including instrument booms)

Engines: 16 thrusters

Rocket: Titan IIIE-Centaur

Launch Date: September 5, 1977

Operator: NASA

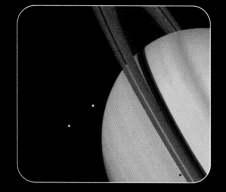

In 1996, *Voyager 1* took this photograph of Saturn and its moons Tethys and Dione.

Generators made electricity from the heat released by radioactive plutonium.

In 1995, *Galileo* was the first spacecraft to orbit Jupiter and study its moons.

Galileo

The radio antenna sends information to Earth, and receives commands, using radio waves.

Voyager 1

Voyager 1 is the most distant human-made object, having left the heliosphere (the bubble of space surrounding the Sun) in 2012.

The radio antenna was 4.8 m (16 ft) wide.

Chang'e 4

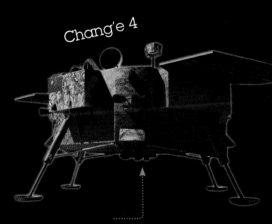

In 2019, this Chinese probe made the first ever soft landing on the far side of the Moon.

NASA astronaut Chris Cassidy photographs Earth from the ISS's Cupola module, built by the European Space Agency.

THE INTERNATIONAL SPACE STATION

The International Space Station (ISS) orbits Earth at a distance of around 410 km (255 miles). A space station is a human-made satellite that is lived on by astronauts. On the ISS, the astronauts do astronomy and weather experiments, as well as studying what happens to living things in space.

The ISS was put together module (or section) by module while in orbit, starting in 1998. To carry out this construction, astronauts did over 1,000 hours of spacewalks (or working outside a spacecraft). They were helped by a large robotic arm called Canadarm2.

The ISS has been continually lived in since 2000, with different astronauts staying for a few weeks or months. After the retirement of the US Space Shuttles in 2011, Russian Soyuz spacecraft were the only way for astronauts to get to and from the space station, until Crew Dragon began flights in 2020 (see page 111).

The ISS is a microgravity environment, where the pull of gravity feels very small, so the astronauts float around. Earth's gravity is pulling on the space station and the astronauts almost as strongly as if they were on Earth. In fact, the spacecraft and its astronauts are all falling toward Earth. Since they are all falling together, the astronauts appear to float. The space station does not actually hit Earth as it is also speeding along at 28,000 km (17,500 miles) per hour, so its "fall" is curved, making it orbit.

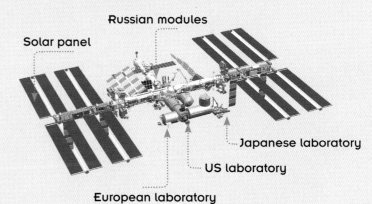

One section of the ISS is operated by Russia, while the rest is shared by astronauts from many countries.

Russian modules

Solar panel

Japanese laboratory

US laboratory

European laboratory

International Space Station

Type: Modular space station

Crew: 6 when full

Size: 109 × 73 m (358 × 239 ft)

Daily Orbits of Earth: 15.5

Launch Date: November 20, 1998

Operator: NASA, Russian State Space Corporation (Roscosmos), Japan Aerospace Exploration Agency (JAXA), European Space Agency (ESA), and Canadian Space Agency (CSA)

ESA astronaut Samantha Cristoforetti works with science equipment on board the ISS.

SPACEPLANES

Like space capsules, spaceplanes are launched into space by rockets that are dropped after use. However, spaceplanes have wings so they can fly back down to Earth's surface. Spaceplanes have never flown higher than a low orbit around Earth. The Space Shuttle has been the most successful spaceplane.

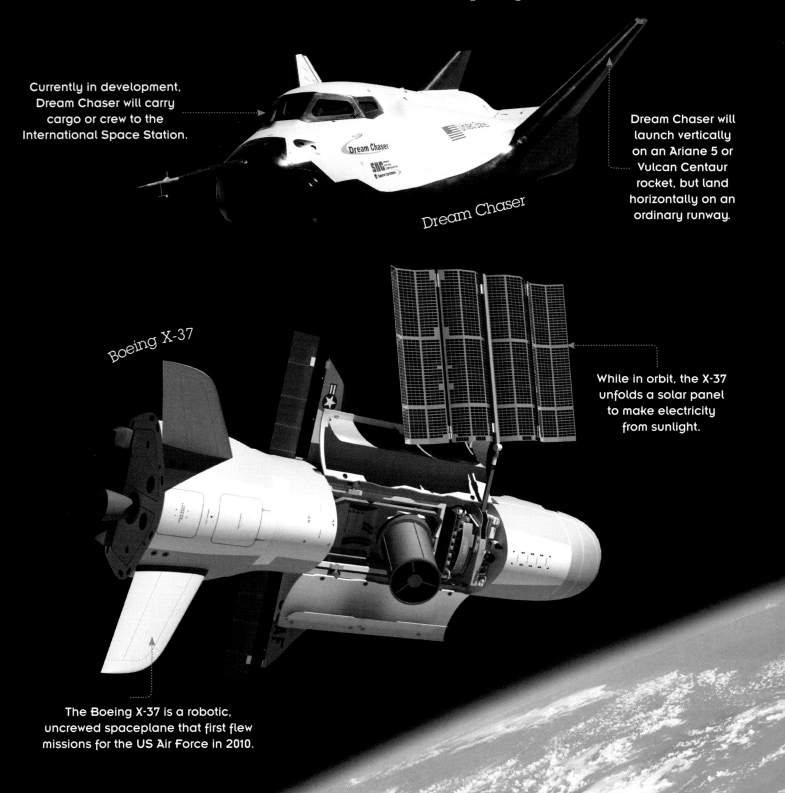

Currently in development, Dream Chaser will carry cargo or crew to the International Space Station.

Dream Chaser will launch vertically on an Ariane 5 or Vulcan Centaur rocket, but land horizontally on an ordinary runway.

Dream Chaser

Boeing X-37

While in orbit, the X-37 unfolds a solar panel to make electricity from sunlight.

The Boeing X-37 is a robotic, uncrewed spaceplane that first flew missions for the US Air Force in 2010.

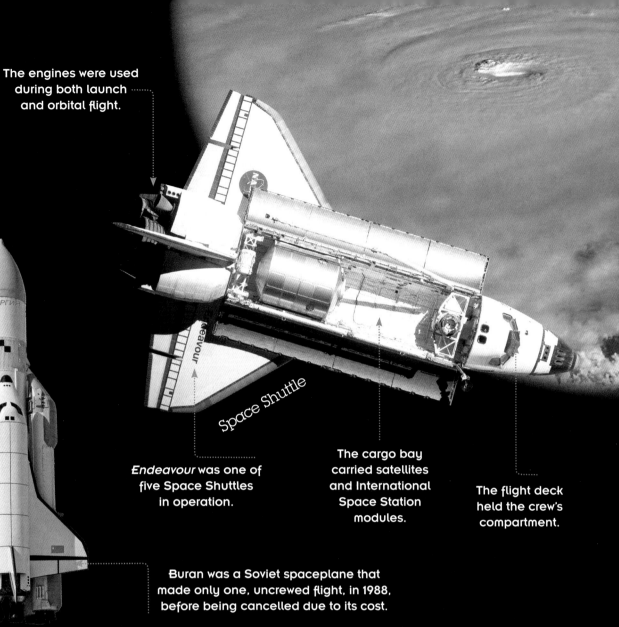

The engines were used during both launch and orbital flight.

The Buran spaceplane was launched by a 2,400,000 kg (5,300,000 lb) Energia rocket.

ЭНЕРГИЯ

CCCP

Space Shuttle

Endeavour was one of five Space Shuttles in operation.

The cargo bay carried satellites and International Space Station modules.

The flight deck held the crew's compartment.

Buran was a Soviet spaceplane that made only one, uncrewed flight, in 1988, before being cancelled due to its cost.

Buran

Space Shuttle

Type: Partly reusable low Earth orbital spaceplane

Seats: Up to 8

Size: 24 m (78 ft) across wings

Engines: 3 RS-25s

Rocket: 2 reusable Solid Rocket Boosters

Launch Date: April 12, 1981

Retirement: July 21, 2011

Operator: NASA

With a Solid Rocket Booster (white) on either side, Space Shuttle *Endeavour* lifts off attached to its fuel tank (red), which supplied fuel to its own engines during launch. The tank and boosters were dropped after launch.

CURIOSITY ROVER

In 2012, *Curiosity* was the fourth rover to land on Mars. Rovers are robotic wheeled vehicles that travel across a planet or moon's surface, taking photos and using instruments to study the rocks and atmosphere. *Curiosity* was lowered by ropes the last 7.5 m (24.6 ft) to Mars's surface from its rocket-powered lander.

Instructions to *Curiosity*, as well as information collected by the rover, are transmitted by radio waves. Due to the time taken for radio waves to travel between Earth and Mars, around 14 minutes, *Curiosity*'s two computers are programmed to carry out its basic activities with little direction from Earth. *Curiosity* is powered by a generator that uses the heat from radioactive plutonium to make electricity. Radioactive materials release energy due to the natural breaking up of their atoms.

One of *Curiosity*'s tasks is to search for signs of water on Mars, both now and in the past. Since life on Earth began in the ocean, signs of rocks worn away by flowing water on Mars's currently dry surface would suggest that life was possible there once.

Curiosity also drills and uses its laser to blast rocks, then tests for signs of tiny life forms. *Curiosity*'s findings suggest that the planet was once more suited to life than it is today, but it has not discovered proof of living things.

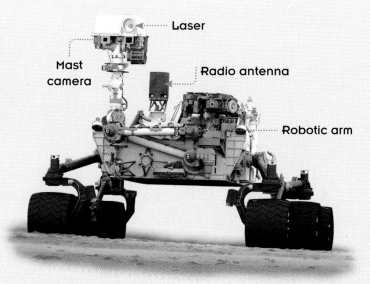

Laser

Mast camera

Radio antenna

Robotic arm

Curiosity weighs 899 kg (1,982 lb), including around 80 kg (180 lb) of scientific instruments.

Curiosity

Type: Mars rover

Size: 2.9 m × 2.7 m (9.5 ft × 8.9 ft)

Equipment: 17 cameras, plus radiation detectors, environmental sensors, and spectrometers that identify materials

Landing Date: August 6, 2012

Landing Site: Gale Crater

Operator: NASA

Curiosity's mast camera took this photograph of the rover's arm, showing its Mars Hand Lens Imager camera (with a round, red dust cover) and motorized wire brush (at right).

Curiosity took this selfie using the Mars Hand Lens Imager camera on its arm, then the arm itself was deleted from the picture by computer.

ASTRONAUTS

Astronauts are the crew members and pilots of spacecraft. The United States and Soviet Union were the first countries to send astronauts into space, from the early 1960s. It was not until 1978 that a citizen of another country reached space. Today, more than 550 people from over 40 countries have made the journey.

Early astronauts were often fighter plane pilots, who had already proved their bravery and quick thinking. Today, crew members are also scientists, doctors, or teachers who can do experiments in space. Until 2002, astronauts were trained and paid only by governments. Since then, some astronauts have been employed by businesses to pilot their spacecraft, such as Crew Dragon. In 2001, millionaire Dennis Tito became the first space tourist, when he paid to stay on the International Space Station for 8 days.

Soviet astronaut Yuri Gagarin (1934–1968) was the first human in space onboard *Vostok 1*.

As his spacecraft launched on April 12, 1961, Gagarin said on his radio: "Off we go! Until soon, dear friends."

Yuri Gagarin

In 1963, Soviet astronaut Valentina Tereshkova (born 1937) became the first woman in space when she orbited the Earth 48 times, alone on board *Vostok 6*.

Mae Jemison

US astronaut Mae Jemison (born 1956) was the first African American woman in space, on board Space Shuttle *Endeavour* in 1992.

Valentina Tereshkova

Some suits are equipped with a TV camera.

The temperature inside the suit can be changed using a valve.

Extravehicular Mobility Unit

During spacewalks, an astronaut wears a spacesuit called an Extravehicular Mobility Unit (EMU), which is attached by a tether to the spacecraft. An EMU is equipped with an oxygen supply, since there is no air to breathe in space. The suit protects an astronaut from extreme temperatures, which range from -155°C (-247°F) in shade to 120°C (248°F) in sunlight. The EMU also keeps out harmful radiation from the Sun, as well as space dust, which can travel as fast as a bullet. During takeoff and landing, a lighter suit and helmet are worn, designed to keep an astronaut safe during changes in temperature and pressure. At other times, astronauts wear comfortable clothes like those worn on Earth.

The suit has 14 layers, including one made of Kevlar, the same material as bulletproof vests.

US astronaut Franklin Chang Díaz (born 1950) is joint record-holder for the most space flights: seven.

Chang Díaz floats in a life raft during a training exercise for exiting a malfunctioning Space Shuttle over the ocean.

Emergency training

It would take at least five spacecraft to carry all the equipment for living on Mars: rovers, living modules, and support modules, where oxygen and water would be made.

MISSION TO MARS

Humans have never set foot on another planet, but the Russian, European, and United States space agencies all have plans to send humans to Mars. Before they can realize this dream, they must build a rocket that could be transported to Mars and then launch from the barren planet for the return journey.

The United States' space agency, NASA, has the most advanced plans to send humans to Mars, during the 2030s. NASA is working on a spacecraft, Orion, that could make the long journey. It will have the same basic structure as Apollo (see page 109) but will be larger and stronger, be powered by solar panels while in space, and could be lived on for a year. Orion could be docked with a habitation module, which might be lived on in Mars's orbit in a similar way to the International Space Station.

Scientists are developing technologies that would let humans live on the surface of Mars, using Mars's own resources to make water and oxygen. Water could be gained by heating the soil until its water evaporates (or turns to gas), then condensing it back into liquid water. Oxygen could be made by splitting water into its parts: oxygen and hydrogen. The fuel to power a rocket for the journey home will be too heavy to carry to Mars, so it must also be made on the planet. All the ingredients for fuel—oxygen, hydrogen, and carbon—can be found on Mars.

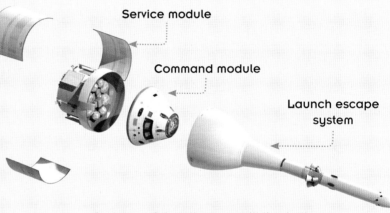

Service module

Command module

Launch escape system

On board Orion, the crew will live in the command module, while the service module provides power, heat, water, and oxygen.

NASA Mission to Mars

Type: Crewed Mars landing mission

Spacecraft: Orion

Rocket: Space Launch System rocket

Launch Date: 2030s

Length of Journey: 7 months to reach Mars

Operator: NASA

This NASA illustration imagines an astronaut growing plants in a greenhouse to provide food on Mars.

GLOSSARY

ASTEROID A small rocky or metal object, over 1 m (3.3 ft) wide, that orbits the Sun.

ASTRONOMER A scientist who studies the planets, stars, and other objects in space.

ATMOSPHERE The gases surrounding a planet or moon, held by its gravity.

ATOM The smallest unit of matter. An atom has a central nucleus, containing particles called protons and neutrons, usually surrounded by one or more electrons.

AXIS An imaginary line through a planet or moon, around which the object rotates.

BLACK HOLE An area of space with such strong gravity that no matter or light can escape from it.

CENTAUR An asteroid-sized object orbiting the Sun in the region of the giant planets.

COMET A small icy object with an elliptical (or stretched) orbit that takes it both close to and far from the Sun.

CORE The inner region of a planet or moon.

COUNTERCLOCKWISE Also known as anticlockwise; the opposite direction from the way the hands of a clock turn.

CRUST The outer layer of a planet or moon.

DAY The time taken for a planet or moon to rotate on its axis until the Sun appears to return to the same position in the sky.

DWARF PLANET An object orbiting a star that is massive enough for its gravity to pull it into a ball, but is not massive enough to clear other objects out of its path.

ECLIPSE When a body such as a star, planet, or moon is obscured by passing into the shadow of another body or by having another body pass between it and the viewer.

ECLIPTIC The plane of Earth's orbit around the Sun.

ELECTRIC CHARGE A property of electrons and protons (see "Atom"). Electrons are negatively charged and protons are positively charged. Negatively and positively charged objects attract each other.

ELECTRIC CURRENT A flow of electrically charged particles.

ELEMENT A pure substance, made of one type of atom, that cannot be broken down into simpler substances.

ENERGY The power to do work that produces light, heat, or motion.

EXOPLANET A planet outside our Solar System.

FLUID A substance that can flow, typically a liquid, but can also be a dense gas or plasma.

GALAXY Millions or billions of stars, as well as gas and dust, that are held together by gravity.

GAS A substance that is not solid, liquid, or plasma, that will expand to fill any container.

GRAVITY A force that pulls all objects and particles toward each other. The greater an object's mass, the greater the pull of its gravity.

HELIUM The second most common and second lightest element in the Universe; helium is a gas at room temperature.

HEMISPHERE Half of a sphere, such as a planet or moon.

HYDROGEN The most common and lightest element in the Universe; hydrogen is a gas at room temperature.

IMPACT CRATER A bowl-shaped dip caused by a collision with an asteroid or other body.

INFRARED A type of energy, given off by objects, that humans can feel as heat.

LIGHT YEAR The distance that light travels in 1 year: 9.46 trillion km (5.88 trillion miles).

MAGNETISM A force caused by the movement of electric charge, resulting in pulling and pushing forces between objects.

MANTLE A layer inside a planet or moon that lies between the core and the crust.

MASS A measure of the amount of matter in an object; sometimes called "weight."

MATTER A physical substance, in the form of a solid, liquid, gas, or plasma.

METEOROID A small rocky or metal object in space, less than 1 m (3.3 ft) wide.

MOLECULE A group of atoms that are bonded together.

MOON A rounded object that orbits a planet.

NAKED EYE Human sight, without the help of a telescope or other device.

NEBULA A cloud of gas and dust.

ORBIT The curved path of an object around a star, planet, or moon.

OXYGEN The third most common element in the Universe; oxygen is a gas at room temperature and is essential for life.

PARTICLE A tiny portion of matter.

PHOTON A particle that carries energy.

PLANE An imaginary flat surface.

PLANET An object orbiting a star that is massive enough for its gravity to pull it into a ball and to push or pull other objects out of its path.

PLASMA An electrically charged gas made of free electrons and atoms that have lost electrons.

RADIOACTIVE Relating to a substance that releases energy as its atoms decay.

RADIO WAVE A type of energy, given off by objects, that can be used for communications.

ROBOTIC Relating to a machine programmed to carry out some of its activities independently.

ROOM TEMPERATURE A comfortable indoor temperature of around 20°C (68°F).

SATELLITE A human-made object that is placed in orbit around a planet or moon.

SOLAR PANEL A device that turns sunlight into electricity.

SOLAR SYSTEM The Sun along with all the planets and other objects in orbit around it.

SOVIET UNION A country that, from 1922 to 1991, included Russia and surrounding nations.

SPACE AGENCY A government organization that works on space exploration.

SPACE PROBE An uncrewed spacecraft.

STAR A glowing ball of plasma, held together by its own gravity.

ULTRAVIOLET A type of energy, given off by objects including the Sun.

WAVELENGTH The distance between the peaks of waves of energy.

YEAR The time taken for a planet to complete one orbit around the Sun.

INDEX